Kate Bush

THE DREAMING

In-depth

Laura Shenton

"I don't see myself as being a publicist for myself but a publicist for my music."

- Kate Bush, 1982

Kate Bush
THE DREAMING

In-depth

Laura Shenton

WP
WYMER
PUBLISHING
Bedford, England

First published in 2021 by Wymer Publishing
Bedford, England www.wymerpublishing.co.uk Tel: 01234 326691
Wymer Publishing is a trading name of Wymer (UK) Ltd

ISBN: 978-1-912782-70-3 (also available as Kindle eBook).

Edited by Jerry Bloom.

Printed and bound in Great Britain by
CMP, Dorset.

A catalogue record for this book is available from the British Library.

Typeset by Andy Bishop / 1016 Sarpsborg
Cover design by 1016 Sarpsborg.
Cover photo © Guido Harari / Pictorial Press Ltd / Alamy Stock Photo.

Contents

Preface

*T*he *Dreaming* is an album that some critics loved to hate. But that's why it is so important.

Kate Bush shot to fame in 1978. Her public image was that of a sweet young woman who sang about Cathy out on the windy moors, full of melancholy and yearning for Heathcliff. It was charming, inoffensive and, although eccentric, subtle enough to come across as endearing or at least, not challenging. Enter *The Dreaming*, Kate Bush's fourth studio album, and all of that changed. And that's why *The Dreaming* matters.

As author of this book, it is my aim to offer an insight into *The Dreaming* in a way that discusses the music in detail in relation to what Kate Bush's creative process was. I want to offer something factual rather than something that is peppered with my own opinion and interpretation of the music. You won't see statements in the lexicon of "this section is in the key of A and it therefore means X" or "I think this lyric means Y." For of course, the beauty of music is often in the ambiguity; it would be futile to throw a lot of my own opinions out there because it won't add anything to the literature if I do that.

The purpose of this book is to look at Kate Bush's fourth album in terms of what she created at the time and how she went about it, as well as the impact that the album made and what its legacy and relevance is today. The facts based on what an artist says about their own work are often more important than the opinion of a music fan offering an enthusiastic narrative. Therefore, throughout this book you're going to see lots of quotes from vintage articles. I think it's important to corroborate such material as there will probably come a time where it is harder to source.

Personally, I think that *The Dreaming* — and indeed all of Kate Bush's albums — are worthy of attention; they all portray something fascinating, both musically and in terms of documenting the career of an artist who hasn't been afraid to try something new and different. It's fair of me to state that here but equally, I promise to be objective in how I present the content in this book; it won't be an exercise in heroine worship.

In the interest of transparency, I have no affiliation with Kate Bush or with any of her associates. This book is based on extensive research and relevant commentary.

KATE BUSH
THE DREAMING

HER NEW ALBUM
AND CASSETTE

ALBUM EMC 3419   EMI   CASSETTE TC/EMC 3419

9

Chapter One

Why The Dreaming?

*T*he *Dreaming* is often regarded as an experimental release on the basis that it draws on musical influences from so many sources. 'There Goes A Tenner' takes inspiration from vintage crime films, the ideas for 'Pull Out The Pin' were based on a documentary about the war in Vietnam, 'The Dreaming' paid strong reference to the plight of Indigenous Australians. 'Get Out Of My House' was inspired by *The Shining*. And then there's 'Houdini', a song about the escape artist.

Across all of the tracks on the album, there is intense emotional exploration, as is the case on 'Sat In Your Lap' and 'Leave It Open'. In terms of instrumentation, *The Dreaming* features didgeridoos, mandolins and uilleann pipes. There are shifts in time signatures and textures as well as the use of polyrhythmic percussion, samples and vocal loops. Of arranging the instrumental and vocal parts in her songs, Kate was quoted in *Electronics & Music Maker* in October 1982; "For most of them I literally just run the tape and learn them in my head, and then translate them. I multi-track my own voice parts, having worked them out first at home. Sometimes I can tell that they're going to work in harmony without having to put one down and then work to that, but it depends, really."

She said in September 1982 on BBC Radio Two; "When I wrote the songs for this album, they felt very different from any of the songs I've written before and it just felt right that I should go the whole way this time. I don't know if I've ever really felt like that before and I don't know if I will in the future, but I really felt that way with these songs, that it was important that I did follow it through with this one."

The Dreaming signified a growing maturity in Kate's music. It took her over a year to make the album and the resulting music was a range of broad ideas weaved together intricately and thoughtfully. In an interview with a German radio station in 1982, when asked if she had changed since the start of her career, Kate replied; "Yes, I think I have. I've learnt a lot so obviously that would change me. But it's good, I'm really glad that I've learnt a lot and there's so much more to learn."

There were so many abstract sounds present on the album that it was considered by some as being more artistic than accessible for the mainstream. Not only that, but some of the songs on *The Dreaming* exceed five minutes and there are none shorter than three minutes, twenty seconds. Kate was quoted in *Zigzag* in November 1982; "It's like a progression. I've never written songs as long as these before. Before they were like three minutes. They all had quite a different process. The idea was to go into the studio each night, put on the rhythm box machine and write something on the spot. Every night I was getting a song, even if it wasn't much good. There'd be an idea I could use in another song. It was all spontaneous initially and became very thought out afterwards. Before, it probably worked the other way. We'd spend ages writing songs and get it all down quick in the studio."

By early 1982, Kate's music was drastically different to that which was popular in the mainstream. Names such as Dollar, Adam Ant, Wham! and The Human League were the in-crowd at the time. Making reliable (and, often predictable) synth pop with hook melodies and lyrics about more run of the mill subjects, they were easier groups for anyone in the music business to promote and anyone in the press to get behind (in an interview with BBC Radio One in 1982, when asked which current bands she thought highly of, Kate said "I really like the Beats, I still like David Bowie, I still like Roxy Music. I like ABC's stuff, Madness, they're great.").

On German radio in 1982, when asked if she felt there was still room for new ideas in commercial music, Kate replied, "Oh, I think so. I think there's always room for them, as long as you can keep open and let them in. I mean, there's just inspiration everywhere, everywhere you look."

She said on BBC Radio Two in September 1982; "I'm a big admirer of Bowie, and people like David Byrne as well. Eno, I think Eno is fantastic. Captain Beefheart, it's a very wide range, really. I think there's a lot of music that I enjoy. But it's mainly people that tend to show strength and originality. People like Bowie, who have gone for something different and they're still standing there."

Pink Floyd was also an influence. Kate told *Melody Maker* in October 1982; "Yes. I've been very much influenced by *The Wall* because I like the way that the Floyd get right into that emotional area and work with sounds as pictures. I think the problem with the film though is that, although as a piece of art it is devastating, it isn't real enough. The whole film is negatively based. Not once during Pink's life is there a moment of happiness, which I know in every human's life there is. Even if you have the shittiest life of all there is always one little moment where you smile for a second or you fall in love with someone and feel happy — maybe only for ten minutes. In *The Wall* there is no compassion and no objectivity at all and I actually think that certain areas of that are destructive."

At the start of Kate's fame, she was on a rollercoaster ride of TV appearances and a 1979 tour that saw her immersed in a whirlwind of glamour and all of the responsibilities that come with being prolific in the music business. It wasn't necessarily something that made her happy though. In *Company* in January 1982, she was quoted as describing the parties as "formal occasions tailor-made for people not to talk to each other".

In the same vein, the care and attention that Kate put into her work was such that in terms of how hard she was working at the time, it was pretty much nonstop. Due to all of this, it wasn't long before the star found herself feeling drained. As she was quoted in the same feature, she was "out of energy, ideas and inspiration."

Released in 1978, Kate's debut album, *The Kick Inside*, featured the song that she is arguably most famous for, 'Wuthering Heights'. The song stayed at the top of the UK singles chart for a whole month. The iconic nature of it was such that it introduced Kate to an unsuspecting public; many didn't know what to make of her. Nevertheless — and perhaps because of how refreshingly different she was — a flurry of hits followed including 'The Man With The Child In His Eyes' and, from her *Lionheart* album released in 1978, 'Hammer Horror' and 'Wow'.

With two albums under her belt, it was then that Kate embarked on a milestone tour. It featured a mesmerising combination of music, dance and theatrical effects. Kate took full responsibility for every element of the show, from staging, lighting and sound to choreography and costumes. It was anything but a small undertaking.

Released in April 1980, her single, 'Breathing', signified a drastic move away from her earlier sound. Her third album, *Never For Ever*, was released in September 1980 to a generally positive reception, along with the single release of 'Army Dreamers'.

Never For Ever was reviewed in *Harrow Midweek* in October 1980; "Kate first wafted on the scene with her superb debut single, 'Wuthering Heights'. Since then she has progressed by leaps and bounds into Britain's premier female rock star. Her records are unique, excellently sculpted examples of inspired imagination and original talent. Her voice can seduce in a breath, provoke with a scream. *Never For Ever* embodies perfectly everything Kate stands for — classic contemporary pop. Her songs are moving and acutely emotional. They range from brooding and melancholy to unrestrained sexuality. 'Delius' and 'Violin' aptly illustrate her versatility, but sometimes the wailing and sweetness of her voice is a little hard to stomach. It is the price of unabashed expression and sincerity. The negative points are, however, greatly outnumbered by the positive and this record will safely notch up Kate Bush's hat-trick of album successes."

Never For Ever marked Kate's first time co-producing an album and by the time it came to making *The Dreaming*, she was fully immersed in the production side of things.

Throughout the early eighties, despite the scale of her success in the UK, Kate had yet to make a substantial impact on US audiences. She did however, have an intensive cult following in Canada which spawned a fan club — so much so that they published a fanzine and held conventions. Despite world domination not being quite the case, for those who had heard of her, it was clear that Kate was talented and versatile as a writer, singer, musician, dancer and producer. She had her own distinctive sound that was constantly evolving and fans were excited to see what she would do next.

By early 1981, Kate was on a brief hiatus, during which she was beginning to get some new song ideas together. The year began with many accolades from the 1980 end of year lists including Best Female Singer (or the equivalent thereof) from both *Record Mirror* and *Melody Maker* (both for the third year running) as well as from *Sounds* and *Smash Hits*. *New Musical*

Express had placed Kate as the second best singer of 1980, with Siouxsie being top.

Change was afoot though, for it is very possible that at this stage in her career, Kate had a strong sense of uncertainty about what might be next. In an interview with *Record Mirror*, she described how unpleasant the comedown was after the dizzying highs of the 1979 tour and that upon the completion of *Never For Ever*, she experienced something similar — but more so. She said in June 1981; "This time it was worse, a sort of terrible introverted depression. The anticlimax of all the work really set in, in a bad way."

Speaking to *Company* in January 1982 Kate also said; "Anyone who is under the illusion that things get easier as you grow older is mistaken."

As a sensitive and thoughtful songwriter, Kate's lyrics told stories and with the innovative use of drum machines, in 1982, it is hardly surprising that her work was often compared to that of Peter Gabriel's. Kate told *Electronics & Music Maker* in October 1982; "The only person I've met who is really into the same kind of approach to playing as I am is Peter Gabriel. He seems to be working "behind the scenes" in a similar way — he's going for the emotional content of the music and lyrics, and he changes his voice. As for my use of local vibrato, if there's a song that needs it, I'll put it in. I have used a choirboy's voice to get a different feeling on 'All The Love'."

Kate's work with Peter Gabriel was evidently pivotal in her own artistic progression. When working with him in 1979 for his eponymous third album released in 1980, it had exposed her to his methods (she provided backing vocals on the tracks, 'No Self Control' and 'Games Without Frontiers').

She told *Melody Maker* in October 1982; "I'd been trying to get some kind of tribal drum sound together for a couple of albums, especially the last one. But really the problem was that

I was trying to work with a pop medium and get something out of it that wasn't part of that set-up. Seeing Peter working in the Townhouse Studio, especially with the engineers he had, it was the nearest thing I'd heard to real guts for a long, long time. I mean, I'm not into rhythm boxes — they're very useful to write with but I don't think they're good sounds for a finished record — and that was what was so exciting because the drums had so much power."

On Gabriel's album, Steve Lillywhite made liberal use of the Fairlight. They also made extensive use of studio processing. The result was an album full of fascinating percussive textures. Kate herself advocated of the ways in which this went on to inspire her music on *The Dreaming*.

Incidentally, 'Sat In Your Lap' was recorded at the Townhouse, the very same studio that Gabriel had used for his third album. Kate said in an interview with BBC Radio One in 1982; "I'd love to work with Peter again, because he's so great. But I don't know, that's something that we would have to see."

As much as from the very early days of her career, Kate was keen to dispute the notion that she was a sex symbol, by the early eighties, there was almost a defiance in her tone towards the subject. Whilst her first two albums featured a high wailing voice and eccentricity that lent themselves to, at times, ridicule and parody, there was still a maturity even in her early work. The subject matters covered by her songs were abstract and often outside of the box; her songs featured characters and ideas beyond the obvious pop music idiosyncrasies, and abundantly so.

It was on *Never For Ever* that Kate first used the Fairlight (a sampling synthesiser, it was in its infancy at the time having only been invented in 1979). In doing so, she was able to bring an enhanced sense of dimension to her music.

Kate told *Keyboard* in July 1985; "I didn't have my own

Fairlight and we had to hire one in." Kate made liberal use of the Fairlight on *The Dreaming*. Whilst she had first used it on *Never For Ever*, it was on *The Dreaming* that it was really used to full capacity.

In response to her use of the Fairlight, Kate said in *Sounds* in October 1982; "It's given me a completely different perspective on sounds. You can put any sound you want onto the keyboard, so if you go 'Ugh!', you can play 'Ugh!' all the way up the keyboard. Theoretically, any sound that exists, you can play. I think it's surprising that with all the gear around at the moment, people aren't experimenting more."

There is an overall cohesion that features on *Never For Ever* across each of the songs on the album. There are moments where the music sounds exotic but every track certainly sounds like it belongs on the album. Kate talked about this in an interview for *Melody Maker* in October 1982; "The last album was very much the starting point for this one. Perhaps the artwork and some of the ideas on *Never For Ever* were misconstrued because although they are very fairytale, on the cover they are meant to depict positive and negative emotions that are very much a part of human beings — that's really what a lot of my songs are about."

The Dreaming took a considerable step away from *Never For Ever*. So, what was the turning point? In response to the statement, "The album *The Dreaming* was quite a radical departure from you previous records," Kate said to *Keyboard* in July 1985; "Yes, I think it is different, but I don't know if it's that different. It's very different from the first two albums, but the third album is where I think we started to get there. I think it was a progression, really. But perhaps not such an obvious one. I think the main difference was connected to my involvement. The more I get involved in the production, then the more I'm going to get exactly what I can out of it.

Therefore, it automatically becomes a more demanding and personal project."

There are certainly some strong similarities between *Never For Ever* and *The Dreaming*. The anti-war theme that features on 'Army Dreamers' certainly carries through on the track, 'Pull Out The Pin'.

By early 1981 *Never For Ever* was starting to gain traction in America. This was particularly the case in parts of the country where Kate had a cult following. For instance, the album was at number twenty-one in the Kansas Foreign Import chart. It was by March that she had some demos down that would go on to form the beginnings of what would become *The Dreaming*. They were done at the studio in East Wickham Farm and were engineered by Del Palmer. Kate said on BBC Radio One in 1982; "I think there's a lot more experimentation on this album. I didn't do any special vocal training, but there were a lot of different ideas when I wrote the songs and put the demos down. And really most of the ideas were in the demos to start with."

By the start of June 1981, Kate hadn't been in the public eye for six months. When asked if she ever worried about taking such long periods of time away from the public eye, Kate said on BBC Radio Two in September 1982; "Yes. I think it worries me a lot. Especially as there seems to be more projects that I do that do take up a lot of time, like maybe a year at a time. But I have to really sit and think, you know, what is the most important thing to me, to stay in the public's eye or to make sure that the work I do is more interesting and that it gets better. And really the only way to make sure that the work gets better is to concentrate on it. So that's definitely my priority."

In late June, the single of 'Sat In Your Lap' was released. It had its first airing on BBC Radio One as part of *Roundtable*, their record review show. Mike Read had initially expressed cynicism about the record: "I heard it earlier in the day and screwed my face up. I'm still undecided. It's certainly unique." As the song faded out, other participants on the show gave their opinions. Rick Wakeman enthused, "Best record I've heard since 'Ashes To Ashes', it sticks out like a sore thumb. Wonderful, it's wonderful."

David Grant (of Lynx fame) said, "Great. It's so different from anything else she's ever done — it's different from *anything* anyone's ever done."

It turned out that Kate had been listening to the broadcast as it happened. During the show, she called up to have a message of thanks passed on.

On *Capital Radio*, TV critic Clive James was played the song and invited to guess who was singing. His response: "I knew straight away it wasn't Ella Fitzgerald. From the doomy dramas I thought it might be Blondie, but then the lyrics got weird and I thought, this has to be Kate Bush... I get bored with a lot of rock music because the second four bars are just like the first four bars. Kate isn't like that. I adore her, she's marvellous... It's not one of her greatest, but good."

By July 1981, the reviews for 'Sat In Your Lap' started to come in. It was certainly a mixed bag. *Record Mirror* urged, "She's whipped up one of her darker, cutting themes... a real knockout after only two listens... buy it!"

New Musical Express called it "aggressive and strident" and "frankly excruciating."

Melody Maker advocated that it was an "arthritic, artistically constipated, out-of-touch travesty that never should have seen the light of day."

Smash Hits put it brutally; "Each and every tackily acted piece of melodramatic Bush rolled into one ghastly mess of a record."

Ouch! Against a backdrop of mixed reviews, Kate embarked on doing a few promotional interviews in which she placed emphasis on the album. At the time, it was expected to be out by November 1981. It wasn't to be though.

In early November 1981, Kate was approached by Michael White, a West End musical producer, he was hoping to cast Kate in the female lead for Gilbert and Sullivan's *The Pirates Of Penzance*. On Broadway, the role had been played by Linda Ronstadt. After giving it some thought, Kate had to turn the offer down on the basis that finishing her still-unreleased album needed to be prioritised. Equally, there are only so many hours in a day.

Kate said in *Company* in January 1982; "I make sure I have time to do everything — I turn down a lot of offers. I know that I need time for my family, my work, my dancing, my practising... When I come out of the studio, it is a bit like being released from prison. I feel like a Martian. In the past, I would have gone straight on to a tour, a stage show or something. Now I decline the offers and spend time at home... While I was working on this album I was offered a part in a TV series. I've been offered other acting roles, but this was the first totally creative offer that has ever come my way. I had to turn it down. I was already committed to the album. Sadly, I don't think that offer will be made again, but you have to learn to let things go, not to hang on and get upset, or to try to do it and then end up making a mess of everything else. It's like wanting to dance in the studio when I'm recording — I want to but I know that I can't because it will just tire me. I wish I had the energy to do everything, but at least I'm healthy and fit."

Kate spoke further about the film work she'd been offered in 1982 when she told a newspaper; "They were always about the rise of a music personality. You know the sort of thing. It's been done time and time before, so it would be a bit boring if I did it. I like films like *Time Bandits* — that was fantastic!"

'Sat In Your Lap' was an important single for Kate because

even in her earlier interviews, she pointed out that she was keen to go for a heavier sound and sometimes found it frustrating that her songwriting method of singing at the piano didn't lend itself to writing a good rock song (yep, even despite 'James And The Cold Gun' and 'Don't Push Your Foot On The Heartbreak').

The smoothness of the piano, she felt, did not lend itself to creating music that had a hard edge to it. 'Sat In Your Lap' signified a move towards music that was driven more by hard rhythm than the flow of a pretty melody.

Kate said in *Electronics & Music Maker* in October 1982; "Since I first started writing, the styles and attitudes have changed. Initially, it was just "me and the piano" and I would write the song until it was completely finished — the lyrics, the tune of one song would take me a couple of weeks. For the last two albums (*Never For Ever* and *The Dreaming*) it's been much looser, and I've been working with rhythm machines as well as the keyboard, and using subject matters already in my head. I'll then make up the music almost on the spot for the subject matter."

In terms of working with rhythm machines, Kate was quoted in the same feature; "It took me quite a while to get used to working with them because they seemed very limiting. I like rhythms to "move", especially in the ballad songs where the tempo would ebb and flow with the words, stopping and slowing down as necessary. Suddenly, having to work with a very strict rhythm, I found it almost impossible at first to tie myself down to the rigid beat. Once I had got used to this, I found that I could work in between the beats."

The 'Sat In Your Lap' single also marked the point at which Kate began moving away from something that she didn't set out to be — a popstar. During in interview with *New Musical Express* in October 1982 she said; "Maybe it's wrong to see me as a pop personality. You're going to keep changing —

'Wuthering Heights' was a story with music and dancing, but I've changed so much since then. The things that the media most remember about me are those things. Some people see that I am changing, but oh, not as many as the people who hang onto those singles. But I am beginning to be seen as an albums artist."

On the Canadian TV show, *The New Music* in 1985, the interviewer made the observation of, "You have been, I think, popularly associated with a very sweet voice, and what you were doing in some places on *The Dreaming* was making very guttural sounds, hoarse and raw, deliberately making your voice crack," Kate replied; "Yes, I find it much more interesting. The first two albums my voice really wasn't capable of doing that. I think my writing and my voice have continually tried to get better, to be able to do something I actually like. And it's very frustrating when you are writing songs and singing them, and you're not enjoying what's coming back. So hopefully, you know, it will be become more pleasurable for me, the actual process, because it is painful to listen to things that sound awful, when you really wanted them to sound good."

On BBC Radio Two in September 1982; Kate said of her music; "Obviously it's more important to me that it pleases me when I'm making it, but when it comes out it's fantastic if other people like it, I mean that's really the reward for all the hard work."

'Sat In Your Lap' gave listeners a taste of how Kate's sound was evolving prior to the release of *The Dreaming*. It includes a range of time signatures: 3/4 and common time with sporadic moments of 2/4 at the end of a phrase ("some say that knowledge is..." and "ho, ho, ho"). It is a busy song with many tracks layered in a way that create a sense of rapidity.

The music video for 'Sat In Your Lap' was directed by Brian Wiseman; it was Kate's first without Keith MacMillan directing. Kate said of her approach to making videos in a TV interview on *Saturday Superstore* in October 1982; "I love doing it. I think the great thing is that it's a growing industry so each time you make a video there's probably new effects around and new techniques... I always used to work with Keith Macmillan, who was a fantastic director, because it's really the director in videos who keeps the direction together. And he was very great, he always used to let me get as involved as I wanted to. And I learnt everything I know from him, really... For a lot of the videos, most of the choreography is mine... I don't think I actually modelled the movements (on a particular dancer), but I've definitely been inspired by particular people and when you see people that are really great, you want to be like them. But I think the thing about dance and music is that it's very much an expression of you from within. So even if you learn to dance or sing, there's always that thing from you, which is really what it's about, I think."

In an interview on *The Old Grey Whistle Test* in 1982, Kate said of her involvement in music videos; "I always work with a director and you have to use an awful lot of people, obviously. But normally the idea comes from me and, because I've written the song, often I've had ideas at an early stage so it's putting them into practice."

When EMI heard the final mixes of *The Dreaming* in March 1982, they were apprehensive. With 'Sat In Your Lap' having been released in 1981, of the remaining tracks, there wasn't one that could be released as a single that would easily fit the AOR mould and commercially, this garnered doubts.

Although they may have heard the album taking shape over the period of its creation, it is plausible that the reality of the financial and economic side of things really came to the fore when they heard the final mix.

For them, as a record company, the uncertainty would have

been multifaceted. First of all, in and of itself, *The Dreaming* was anything but middle of the road and secondly, it went drastically against the public's expectations of Kate based on her previous releases. It was a far cry from the sweet gentle melodies of 'The Man With The Child In His Eyes' and the wailing characterisation of Cathy in 'Wuthering Heights'.

Kate told *Zigzag* in November 1982; "I think I've definitely changed a lot since it all started happening, the last three years. You can't not change. I think in some ways I don't worry about things so much, but in other areas I probably worry much more. I can't work it out. Maybe I'm a bit harder."

In a newspaper interview she also said "I couldn't go on forever as the little girl with the 'hee-hee' squeaky voice."

When asked about 'Wuthering Heights' in an interview with BBC Radio Two in September 1982, Kate said; "I think there were a lot of different reactions, some people really liked it, some people really didn't, and other people found it very amusing. For me, really, I just see it as a phase of my writing where I was just into playing around with that kind of range. And I find it changes, as far as I'm concerned that's an old style for me now. But of course a lot of people still see that as being me now. But that's just part of the time situation where for a lot of people they will always think of me as 'Wuthering Heights' and nothing else... And also of course it was the most successful single I've had, so that obviously does tend to stick in people's minds a lot. But as far as I'm concerned, I feel like I'm changing, hopefully with each album I do. It's especially my voice. I mean, in a way I'm still quite fond of some of the flavours of the old albums and some of the songs, but, my voice, it always sounds so young to me, because I feel that it's changing all the time."

Perhaps EMI were as surprised as the unsuspecting public when they first heard the finished version of *The Dreaming*.

Nick Launay (engineer) was quoted in *Uncut* in January 2012;: "I don't remember anybody from EMI coming down. They were kept at arm's length. There was basically her, the musicians she chose, and an engineer. On a technical level, making that record had no rules, we could try everything that came to mind. We were both in the same place: 'I wonder what this does?' It was an approach of plugging things in, seeing what it did, and working out how you use that to manipulate the instrument you're playing. The sound on 'The Dreaming', this metallic sound, very dreamy and surreal, is actually a guitar and a piano going into a harmoniser — the note goes up and up and up in octaves until it's so high you can't hear it. We used that on quite a few songs."

EMI may have been right to have concerns, not just in terms of Kate's music but in general. In the early eighties, sales of records were low across the board compared to what they had been. Kate said on German radio in 1982, "I think the interesting thing is that although the sales are down, there's an incredible amount of really good new material. I can't remember the last time there were so many top acts having their albums out, and the quality being so high."

From a financial perspective, it is understandable as to why EMI may have had their doubts. The cost of making the album would have made a big impact on potential profit from it. In an interview with BBC Radio Two in September 1982, Kate was asked, "I know, Kate, it has taken you virtually a whole year to write it and record it and produce it, indeed. So how often can you have the luxury of devoting a year to an album?" Her response: "Oh, well, that is the first time. I think the thing that happens is each time I do an album it takes me longer and with this album it was very demanding and there were lots of things that I wanted to do so I knew it was going to take a long time. But it is a luxury, really, to be able to spend that amount of time in the studio... I think it's the hardest thing I've ever done. It's definitely the most involved thing I've ever done... When you're working on songs they very much dictate what you should do to them, so in many ways I was just trying to make the songs as best as they could be and they were very much demanding what should be done to them."

Could EMI's doubts have been a self-fulfilling prophecy on their part though? For instance, when 'There Goes A Tenner' was released as a single, it wasn't even plugged to Radio One! On balance though, whilst a number of fans complained that *The Dreaming* and indeed Kate wasn't best supported by EMI at the time, the fact remains that the album and every track on it was a commercial risk and realistically, there is no getting away from that.

'There Goes A Tenner' was the only single of Kate's to flop. On the B-side of the single was 'Ne T'enfuis Pas'; sung in French, it was Kate's first song to be recorded in a language other than English.

On balance, it comes across that Kate was more motivated by making albums than singles. She told *New Musical Express* in October 1982; "I think I've always seen myself as someone who writes songs that go on an album. If there are any singles among them, then they can be chosen for that. But apart from 'Wuthering Heights', I was always an album-orientated artist. Even if my singles are more remembered... Each album is like a rocket. I build it up as much as I can and see how high it goes. I'm never aware of any commercial value. I never sit down to write a single. Whenever I write, I'm challenging myself in some area. Everyone who creates something considers themselves an artist in some way, don't they?... I'm not interested in making singles. Maybe I will make some "singles" one day."

Although *The Dreaming* was ready to go by May, it wouldn't see a release until the September (even the release of *Never For Ever* had been delayed for four months by EMI due to — what they regarded as — marketing reasons. This must have been frustrating considering how hard Kate worked to meet an earlier deadline).

This did afford Kate some time for rest and recuperation though and it saw her taking some time out in Jamaica. It was rumoured that around this time, publishers Sidgwick and Jackson were hoping to publish a Kate Bush autobiography but with everything else going on, the release date was delayed to spring 1983. In late June 1982, Kate only made one public appearance — albeit an immensely subtle one — as she sat in the audience for The Rolling Stones' gig at Wembley.

Kate told *Electronics & Music Maker* in October 1982; "The LP for me has been quite fulfilling. I feel I have made a step forward, which is always great for one artistically, obviously. And I suppose one of the things that I do feel pleased about is perhaps that I feel we've got a sense of the emotional value from each song to have come across in some way. It was very emotionally demanding, especially some of the tracks, because of the subject matter. It's taken a year to put together, with a lot of studio time taken up. It was actually finished in May, but we felt it was better to release it in the autumn — but it's really such a long time to wait."

'The Dreaming' single was released in late July 1982. Alongside the official review copies that were made available, there was no EMI press release. Instead, there was a handwritten note from Kate supplied with each that read: "The Dreaming — The Aboriginals are not alone in being pushed out of their land by modern man, by their diseases or for their own strange reasons. It is very sad to think they might all die. 'The Dreaming' is the time for Aboriginals when humans took the form of animals, when spirits were free to roam and in this song as the civilised begin to dominate, the "original ones" dream of dream-time."

Well, on balance, it was certainly different. *Record Mirror* wrote of the single in July 1982 "They say this one grows on you, but to me it sounds like one hell of a jumble… Very ambitious, but until I've heard it another fifty times, I haven't a clue."

Sounds called it "a churning, chundering chant that's soporific in the extreme."

Melody Maker considered; "The weirdest damn record I've ever heard… primitive and relentless and then in comes Kate's fearsome twisted voice — it put the fear of God in me."

Smash Hits called it "the oddball single to end all oddball singles. Very bizarre."

Positively though, *New Musical Express* advocated that the single was "bold and good" whilst *Hot Press* asserted that it was "a brilliantly conceived and executed sound picture by a woman who hasn't gotten half enough recognition."

It was reviewed in the *Liverpool Echo*; "Antipodean adenoids from Kate on this very strange single. Has to be heard with the headphones jammed full on to appreciate the true beauty of the beast... Still, it should generate sufficient airplay to chart."

Overall though, radio airplay of 'The Dreaming' was sporadic and consequently, plans for a 12" version of the single were rapidly abandoned.

With Kate having co-produced *Never For Ever* with Jon Kelly, *The Dreaming* was the first album on which she opted to produce on her own. With maximum control over the project, she had the scope to experiment with production techniques which allowed her to blend a range of musical styles and ideas together.

Engineer Paul Hardiman recalled to *Uncut* in January 2012; "She wanted to produce herself, to move on from possibly some rather safe studio sounds and just experiment. She had been building up to this, but EMI were very reluctant for her to have total control after what had been a successful run of albums."

Kate said in *Poppix* in summer 1982; "After the last album, *Never For Ever*, I started writing some new songs. They were very different from anything I'd ever written before — they were much more rhythmic, and in a way, a completely new side to my music. I was using different instruments, and everything was changing; and I felt that really the best thing to do would be to make this album a real departure — make it completely different. And the only way to achieve this was to sever all the links I had had with the older stuff. The main link was engineer Jon Kelly. Every time I was in the studio Jon was there to help me, so I felt that in order to make the stuff different enough I would have to stop working with Jon. He really wanted to keep working with me, but we discussed it and realised that it was for the best."

She said in an interview with BBC Radio One in 1982; "I did enjoy producing the album, it wasn't easy at all. But yes, I did enjoy it because I was pleased with the result. I don't know about producing other artists, I don't know."

It come across that when Kate opted to produce *The Dreaming*, her decision was perhaps based on wanting to be able to meld her creative ideas with the technical scope of what could be done in the studio. She explained to *Electronics & Music Maker* in October 1982; "I like to be involved with everything that's going on the album, and I do have a lot of interest in the technical problems that crop up as well — that's really happened over the last couple of years. In a way, the technical side of what is happening is as inspirational as what you get out of it."

In response to the question of "The new album took over a year to record, is this due to the fact that you have been involved one hundred percent in its production?" Kate said on BBC Radio One in 1982; "Yes, I think that's certainly contributed to the fact that it's taken a long time. But there are a lot of other things as well. The songs themselves were very demanding, especially emotionally. And they seemed to be requiring more special sounds, new treatment, that sort of thing. So it was harder to find sounds that were right and it took longer to get ideas manifested. And also, I was having to work between three or four studios in order to be able to get the time to make sure that the impetuous was carried on and the album was finished. Because I was making an album at the same time a lot of other people were and obviously everybody wanted to use the same top studios in London, so I was having to move around a lot, which was hard."

The interviewer added, "I would have thought if you're going to take that long over an album, recording things, that it must be hard to keep the interest up in some tracks, 'cause you may record or write a song — you think 'that sounds terrific' and then sort of the whole thing kind of rescinds over the few weeks and you think, 'well maybe that wasn't a great song'."

Kate's reply: "That really was my biggest problem. I mean there are all kinds of problems like lack of confidence and worrying about things, but the real problem was that I was starting to lose interest in the songs and I was starting to worry about the songs, wondering, as you were just saying, if they were still as good as I thought they were when I actually wrote them. And you just have to be working with really good people who keep saying 'it's great, don't worry it sounds great.' And you just keep doing it and maybe a few days later you think 'yeah, it's not so bad but I don't know about this one'."

The recording for *The Dreaming* had started around the time that *Never For Ever* was released. The first demo of 'Sat In Your Lap' has been laid down in September 1980. In particular, Kate felt inspired after attending a Stevie Wonder concert. Kate said of 'Sat In Your Lap' on BBC Radio Two in September 1982; "I went to see the Stevie Wonder gig and it was incredible, it was really good. And the next night I went into our home studio and wrote the song in a couple of hours and that was it, one of the quickest songs I've ever written."

Kate wrote in the *Kate Bush Club* magazine in October 1982; "I already had the piano patterns, but they didn't turn into a song until the night after I'd been to see a Stevie Wonder gig. Inspired by the feeling of his music, I set a rhythm on the Roland and worked in the piano riff to the high-hat and snare. I now had a verse and a tune to go over it but only a few lyrics like 'I see the people working...' so the rest of the lyrics became 'na-na-na' or words that happened to come into my head. I had some chords for the chorus with the idea of a vocal being ad-libbed later. The rhythm box and piano were put down, and then we recorded the backing vocals 'Some say that knowledge is...' Next we put down the lead vocal in the verses and spent a few minutes getting some lines worked out before recording the chorus voice. I saw this vocal being sung from high on a hill on a windy day. The fool on the hill, the king of the castle — 'I must admit, just when I think I'm king.' The idea of the demos was to try and put everything down as quickly as possible. Next came the brass. The CS80 is still my favourite synthesiser next to the Fairlight, and as it was all that was available at the time, I started to find a brass sound. In minutes I found a brass section starting to happen, and I worked out an arrangement. We put the brass down and we were ready to mix the demo. I was never to get that CS80 brass to sound the same again — it's always the way. At the Townhouse the same approach was taken to record the master of the track. We put down a track of the rhythm box to be replaced by drums, recording the piano at the same time. As I was producing, I would ask the engineer to put the piano sound on tape so I could refer to that for required changes. This was the quickest of all the tracks to be completed, and was also one of the few songs to remain contained on one twenty-four track tape instead of two!"

When 'Sat In Your Lap' was released in June 1981, it peaked at number eleven in the UK singles chart. The other songs that would come to make up *The Dreaming* took longer to develop thereafter. It was actually as part of a somewhat last-minute decision that 'Sat In Your Lap' made it onto *The Dreaming*.

Kate told *Poppix* in summer 1982; "We weren't going to put it on initially, because we thought it had been a single such a long time ago, but a lot of people used to ask me if we were putting 'Sat In Your Lap' on the album and I'd say no, and they would say 'Oh why not?' and they'd be quite disappointed. So, as the album's completion date got nearer and nearer, I eventually relented. I re-mixed the track and we put it on. I'm so glad I did now, because it says so much about side one, with its up-tempo beat and heavy drum rhythms — it's perfect for the opening track."

It was over the summer of 1981 that Kate worked at Abbey Road Studios and Odyssey Studios. It was during this time that she worked with the Irish band Planxty and The Chieftains in Dublin. The long days spent in the studio were such that Kate then made the decision to take a break from working on the album.

The break began in late 1981 but by January 1982 Kate was back at Advision Studios laying overdubs and other final touches onto her work. This continued through into May 1982. The album was in very early stages in January 1982, when Kate was quoted that month in *Company*; "At the moment it hasn't got a title. It has been very hard to produce because all the studios are so incredibly booked up, and because I wanted to use one engineer only. This is the first album that I have actually produced myself. Inevitably, this has meant a great deal more responsibility for me. But it is a responsibility I like; I think that as soon as you get your hands on the production, it becomes your baby. That's really exciting for me, because you do everything for your own child. And I have been forced to think harder about what is good and what is not so good... I like to leave all my options open until the last minute so that I'm really sure — like about the title of an album, for instance. I'm taking a complete break from recording at the moment, going over songs, tightening up lyrics and tunes, not going near the studio. I've worked on this album so intensely for so long that I seemed to be losing sight of my direction. I really wasn't sure what to do next — and that has never happened to me before."

After the album's release, Kate said in *Zigzag* in November 1982; "The title actually came last. It always does. It's the most difficult thing to do. I tried to get a title that would somehow say what was in there."

The Dreaming was released in September 1982 following the second single — the title track. Commercially the single didn't do too well, peaking only at number forty-eight in the UK. In an interview with BBC Radio One in 1982, Kate said of 'The Dreaming' single when asked how she felt about its chart position; "Obviously I was a bit disappointed, but it's just the way it goes, really. I think what was more disappointing was the fact that we'd made a video for it and we weren't able to get it shown, and we'd put a lot of work into it. But really what concerns me is the album, much more than the singles. So it's not a problem really... I think the problem is that often there aren't publicity campaigns for singles, because they don't actually seem to do much good, and that's the problem. Often a single is kept under its own weight... And there's not really that much you can do."

When Kate was interviewed on the TV show *Pebble Mill At One* in October 1982, she answered the questions about 'The Dreaming' single with candour and courage; "It's not really a commercial song at all and I think that's rather lovely… The direction I'm going in with my art is the way *I* want to go because, for me, it's a little deeper, it's got more meaning. It's not so poppy I suppose, but of course, maybe that won't be so widely accepted, especially in the singles chart, where it seems that things do have to be obvious really to stand a good chance of getting places."

When asked if she regretted going with 'The Dreaming' as the first single to be released in support of the album, Kate said on BBC Radio One in 1982; "No, not at all. If I was to make the same choice, I would. I would go for that same record, you know what I mean? If I had to put the first single out again I would go for that one, I'm very happy."

Despite initial apprehensions, the album got to number three in the UK. It remained in the chart for ten weeks. Kate said in an interview with BBC Radio One in 1984; "The main thing I heard was "uncommercial"… the label that the press and the record company put on it… But for an uncommercial record to go straight in at number three in the charts seems ironic to me."

In November 1982, 'There Goes A Tenner' was released as the next single from *The Dreaming*. It was the only single of Kate's not to get into the UK top one hundred. In Europe though, 'Suspended In Gaffa' was released as a single instead. Also, 'Night Of The Swallow' was released as a single in Ireland in November 1983. As a single, 'Suspended In Gaffa' did pretty well in the places it was released.

Despite the fact that *The Dreaming* didn't have the success that her debut album did, it was the first album of Kate's to make a dent in the US Billboard 200 chart. It is considered by some that the rise of college radio accounted for this at the time. Following this, in 1984, *Lionheart* was given a belated released in the US.

On German radio in 1982, the interviewer commented, "Are you surprised about your success in England because a lot of artists are very successful in Germany, wherever — Europe, but not in England. You are successful in England and in the rest of Europe." Kate replied; "It makes me very happy. And I think especially because it's my homeland. That really means a lot to me because I live in England. And to see that being reflected amongst my friends and where I live, it's really special."

All turbulence accounted for, *The Dreaming* is arguably a product of a tremendous amount of thought and innovation. So much so, that it is important to consider what it meant for Kate Bush as an artist at that stage in her career.

BUSHY TALES

KATE BUSH TELLS KAREN SWAYNE ABOUT HER LATEST DREAM

Steve Rapport

Chapter Two

The Making Of The Dreaming

Kate collaborated with several sound engineers across the making of *The Dreaming*. It was to the creative advantage of the album — although the reasoning behind it was also of an ergonomic nature.

In October 1982, Kate wrote for the *Kate Bush Club* magazine; "I have had a lot of help with this album. I never could have done it alone, and each person has contributed something very special. We worked between several studios, getting time where we could at the studios with the facilities we required, eventually settling in at Advision Studios, where we finished all the overdubs and mixed the tracks. We also worked at the Townhouse and the Odyssey, and at Abbey Road Studios, where all the backing tracks were recorded. I used several engineers, working with Hugh Padgham, Nick Launay, Haydn Bendall and Paul Hardiman. All of them were very important and all played major parts in how the album has ended up sounding. Hugh worked on 'Sat In Your Lap', 'Get Out Of My House', and 'Leave It Open'. Hugh was a lot of fun to work with and as the first engineer on the album, he started it off in a very productive and positive way. I met Hugh when I had the pleasure to sing some backing vocals for Peter Gabriel, and I was very impressed with the sounds and the creative atmosphere. Hugh has worked with The Police, Genesis and XTC, just to mention a few. We felt very pleased with the backing tracks and were excited at the results; however, Hugh was too busy to continue, and so I worked with Nick Launay, who had been trained by Hugh. Nick worked on 'Houdini', 'All The Love', 'There Goes A Tenner', 'The Dreaming' and 'Suspended In Gaffa'. The majority of the backing tracks were recorded with Nick at the Townhouse. We were working through the warm summer last year, and much dedication was required from all to stay in the studio all day without succumbing to the sun. Nick is a very young engineer and has already worked with Public Image, Phil Collins and John Martyn. Again there was a great working relationship and we were all sad that Nick was too busy to continue and that the time at the Townhouse had run out. I moved on to Abbey Road, working with Haydn Bendall. I met him on the last album when I was working with Jon Kelly. Haydn was co-producing Sky and I found him a very patient and understanding engineer. Haydn also engineered Roy Harper's last album and among many other artists, helps up and coming writers to get their ideas securely onto tape, often securing record contracts at the same time. Haydn worked on 'Night Of The Swallow' and 'Pull Out The Pin'. Our assistant engineer Danny Dawson, affectionately known as Dan-Dan, became part of the working team on the two tracks, and it was really enjoyable. It always is fun when you work with nice people. The two tracks are finished and Haydn's time runs out too, so... I find Paul Hardiman, with a lot of help from Hugh Padgham. Paul has worked with a great variety of acts, from Slade to Keith Emerson and Soft Cell. We worked at Odyssey Studios up until Christmas (1981), and by then Paul and I had a great working relationship. I felt I could communicate with him very easily and he could get the sounds I needed to hear, very quickly."

She continued, "We ran out of time at Odyssey and Paul suggested Advision, studios he knew from experience. He took me around there one afternoon on a Sunday. The studio was deserted and we went down to a small control room that proved to have a brilliant sound. We were sitting listening to tapes at full blast and I was falling in love with the room when the door slowly opened and a rather anxious looking studio manager edged around the door. He saw Paul and sighed with relief and explained how he'd expected a gang of thugs to be tearing up the studio while listening to tapes of their choice — as far as he had known, the studio was empty. We asked him if there would be any time for us to use the studio, and the three weeks we booked were to turn into more like three months. Paul and I were very excited about settling in to one studio, and Paul had some wonderful effects for sounds that he'd put away for a rainy day. I'm pleased there was a lot of rain to come. Although all the engineers were invaluable, Paul was of special value. He became a constant companion during the album and I would often ask his advice, knowing I would get an honest answer. He is also a very funny man, so he kept us all laughing — donning silly hats and pulling funny faces. At Advision we met Dave Taylor — he was the assistant engineer, and he worked with us for months until the album was finished and mixed. Dave was also the maintenance engineer, and on quite a few nights, when we went home to bed, he would be up all night twiddling inside machines or trying to figure out why the digital machines weren't working. Every night we ate takeaway food, watched the evening news and returned to the dingy little treasure trove to dig for jewels. Now it's all finished, I think of the beginning. Twenty demos, ten of which became the album. In these demos all the moods and sounds were captured, and all the way through the album these demos were referred to. Often the session would stop, we'd dig out the quarter inch tape of the track we were working on, and with the original flavour and sounds strong in our heads, the session would begin again. In many ways it would have been interesting to have used the demos as masters, they were so spontaneous. Del Palmer engineered all the demos and every night he would sit up in the cramped little control room, getting different sounds for each track. He sat through hours of harmonies and takes of lead vocals, replying 'I'm not bored' as many times as there were cups of tea, and nodding 'Yeah, Kate, I think it sounds great!', a phrase to be echoed by Hugh, Haydn, Paul — Bless you all."

Many of the rhythms on *The Dreaming*, especially the title track, came more from vocal rhythms; they weren't particularly keyboard-based. Kate told *Keyboard* in July 1985; "That's not a keyboard-based song at all. It's very much based on Aboriginal music that I'd been able to hear. That was actually an idea I'd had since the third album. I knew I wanted to write a song that was about abuses — the Aborigines, the Indians, these tribes whose countries had been taken away from them by so-called civilised man. I wanted it to be based around the Aboriginal style of music. Their music says so much to me about space, earth, and living on the land. So the whole thing is based around the didgeridoo. I have a rough sample in my Fairlight, and I sort of worked out ideas from that. Then we got people in and pieced all the other sounds together. It was quite a visual song, because you could see so many things that suggested to you where to place sounds. I think it would be insulting to the instrument to suggest that the Fairlight could do it better — I don't know if you realise the sort of circular breathing technique that's involved in playing it... I think that the combination of very acoustic real sounds and very hard electronic sounds is fabulous. I like to create contrasts and extremes for the atmosphere that you're building around a particular song."

There was a greater emphasis on rhythm in *The Dreaming*. Kate said to *Zigzag* in November 1982; "The rhythm box did that. It took me a while to get used to it. I kept moving with it instead of in and out of it, which was restricting me. Now it seems so natural... It's hard for me to really get power coming across. It's the first time I've had to get that much power, because the songs were demanding it. It was hard."

The emphasis on percussion and rhythm on *The Dreaming* wasn't such that there was no thought for harmony in Kate's songwriting. In response to the question of "Do you work up from the root and then add the third and the fifth?" In an interview with *Electronics & Music Maker* in October 1982 she said; "No, I never work that way — I just go for what sounds right, and never think technically about thirds and fifths, because very often I think fourths and sixths could be better. I like to use parallel movement for a more medieval feel, and I also sing unrelated notes against the harmony — say, dropping semitones — which helps to create a lot of tension. But I do try to avoid thinking about the technical things when I'm working — it's afterwards that I like to think about those aspects. For the male voice parts, I just sing to them what I want them to do, and I tell them the particular phraseology and timing. Then they go out and do it, while I oversee it in the mixing room. I'm lucky in that they're not really session singers, but more friends with good voices."

Regarding the counterpoint in Kate's songs, she was quoted in the same feature; "It's something that I find works in layers. For example, normally the song, with its basic tune and chords, would be down, and then, as things start to go on more to the track, I can just hear holes that need to be filled in a certain way. Sometimes I would be doing this with tapes at home or during a meal break at the studio. I'd go round and round parts of the tape and sing with it... For the actual tune; whilst any additional harmonies would be added afterwards using a tape with the basic piece on it. I use a Revox half-track machine to sing along with — I never put it down though at this stage — I just sing with it to see if it works. Really, it's for playback, to help me, and I would use an eight-track studio for demos. I've also been using the Teac Portastudio 144, which I find useful... It depends completely on the song. Whatever the song's saying, then that little hole in there that's waiting for a harmony needs something special."

For the recording of 'The Dreaming', Kate employed the skills of Rolf Harris and Percy Edwards. In an interview on *The Old Grey Whistle Test* in 1982, Kate said of Rolf; "He is a very good didgeridoo player, which is why we used him."

Percy Edwards was brought in to do the sound effects on 'The Dreaming', Kate said in the same interview; "I knew that in the choruses we wanted to create a feeling of the landscape, and obviously there are a lot of Australian animals and the sounds are very reminiscent of the environment. And of course Percy could come along and give us a selection of at least ten different Australian animals... I think he's made a study of nearly any animal that's alive and he's very unique. There is no one else really who's doing what he does."

Elsewhere Kate also said; "The wonderful thing about Percy is that he can look like the animal he's trying to impersonate. You should see him when he does a gorilla. He's been impersonating animals for years, and he told me that when he started there were no records with animal sounds, so he went to the zoo. I've always wanted to meet him — he's such a fascinating man."

Of 'The Dreaming', Kate wrote for the *Kate Bush Club* magazine in October 1982; "We started with the drums, working to a basic Linn drum machine pattern, making them sound as tribal and deep as possible. This song had to try and convey the wide open bush, the Aborigines — it had to roll around in mud and dirt, try to become a part of the earth. "Earthy" was the word used most to explain the sounds. There was a flood of imagery sitting waiting to be painted into the song.

The Aborigines move away as the digging machines move in, mining for ore and plutonium. Their sacred grounds are destroyed and their beliefs in Dreamtime grow blurred through the influence of civilisation and alcohol. Beautiful people from a most ancient race are found lying in the roads and gutters. Thank God the young Australians can see what's happening. The piano plays sparse chords, just to mark every few bars and the chord changes. With the help of one of Nick Launay's magic sounds, the piano became wide and deep, effected to the point of becoming voices in a choir. The wide open space is painted on the tape, and it's time to paint the sound that connects the humans to the earth, the didgeridoo. The didgeridoo took the place of the bass guitar and formed a constant drone, a hypnotic sound that seems to travel in circles... I've never experienced a sound quite like it before. It was like a swarm of tiny velvet bees circling down the shaft of the didgeridoo and dancing around in my ear. It made me laugh, but there was something very strange about it, something of an age a long, long time ago. Women are never supposed to play a didgeridoo, according to Aboriginal laws; in fact there is a didgeridoo used for special ceremonies, and if this was ever looked upon by a woman before the ceremony could take place, she was taken away and killed, so it's not surprising that the laws were rarely disobeyed. After the ceremony, the instrument became worthless, its purpose over. It's interesting how some songs attract lots of ideas — this was definitely one of them, and because of the amount of ideas in this song, it made me concentrate on others, so they would not be neglected or left behind. Percy Edwards was among the ideas for this song, and he too was a real pleasure to work with. He really is the only man who imitates the voices of animals to the extent that he does and is greatly respected for his talents. It is so beautiful to watch him burst into birdsong in a studio in the middle of London. I had images of him waking with the dawn chorus, taking part with blackbirds, the sparrows, the thrushes, but we were in the studio with Percy, and there was work to do, so he became sheep, dingoes and Australian magpies. The light grew dim and we were out in the bush on a warm windy night by the light of Percy, our fire. Percy is a true professional, and he kept us all in awe with his wonderful ways. He was, however, a little upset by the treatment of the kangaroos, but after Paddy and I explained it was the only way to get the sound we wanted, he completely understood the situation and tried to communicate to the kangas what they had to do. The only problem was he couldn't remember the kanga word for "dang" so he worked on "boing" with a "D".

In an interview with BBC Radio One in 1982, when asked to clarify the meaning of the words in 'The Dreaming', Kate said, "'The Dreaming', which is also known as 'Dreamtime', was the time for the Aborigines more or less at the beginning of creation when animals and humans took the same form. It was very magical and it's of incredible religious significance to them. And that's what it's about."

She said of 'The Dreaming' on Radio One in August 1982; "Really it's a song about the Australian Aborigines who've been treated incredibly badly by the white man... but it doesn't just apply to Aborigines, I think we've done our fair share of being cruel to people. And certainly to the red Indians in America, all this sort of thing... thank God the Aborigines are getting themselves together again. They're all starting to grow, there are much more of them now then there were even a few years ago."

Elsewhere she said; "I think there's about two thousand Aborigines left. Unfortunately their lands are where you find plutonium, a very rare metal which is used in bombs. They're beautiful people... One day I want to go and see the outback for myself. I'm sure it's everything that I've dreamed about."

In an interview with BBC Radio One in 1982, Kate said of the voice that features at the end of 'The Dreaming'; "It is Aborigine. And it's a lyric from a song called 'Airplane! Airplane!' And it's very strange because it's one of the first Aboriginal songs about airplanes which were coming from the civilised Australians."

In an interview on *The Old Grey Whistle Test* in 1982, Kate spoke of a trip she took to Australia; "Four years ago, it was just a promotional trip but I managed to talk to the young Australian people about Aborigines and their knowledge of them, if they ever met them. And they told me all about the kangaroos and what a nuisance they are, how they have the big crash barriers on the front... I picked up a feeling for what it was like from being there so, yes, it was quite inspirational."

Kate said of 'The Dreaming' on BBC Radio Two in September 1982; "It was inspired years ago by Rolf Harris' 'Sun Arise'. And, although when I heard it then — I was probably about six — it never occurred to me that I would write a song inspired by it, that is in fact what happened 'cause it's been in my head ever since."

She told *Zigzag* in November 1982; "I knew the beat from 'Sun Arise' and Aborigine music, so we just ripped that off, used what was already there ethnically. Rolf just came in and did didgeridoo."

Kate told *Poppix* in summer 1982; "Years ago my brother bought 'Sun Arise' and I loved it, it was such a beautiful song. And ever since then I've wanted to create something which had that feel of Australia within it. I loved the sound of the traditional Aboriginal instruments, and as I grew older, I became much more aware of the actual situation which existed in Australia between the white Australian and the Aborigines, who were being wiped out by man's greed for uranium. Digging up their sacred grounds, just to get plutonium, and eventually make weapons out of it. And I just feel that it's so wrong — this beautiful culture being destroyed just so that we can build weapons which maybe one day will destroy everything, including us. We should be learning from the Aborigines, they're such a fascinating race. And Australia — there's something very beautiful about that country... The song was originally going to be called 'Dreamtime', which is the name the Aborigines gave to a magic time before man was man as he is today — when man was an animal and could change shape. This magical time was also known as The Dreaming to the Aborigines, so I thought it would be an ideal title for the song. 'The Dreaming' is such a strong title, too: "dreaming" on its own means little, but with "the" in front of it, it takes on a whole new meaning."

When asked whether the title track formed the actual cornerstone of the LP, Kate said in *Melody Maker* in October 1982; "No. The thing about all my album titles is that they're usually one of the last things to be thought of because it's so difficult just to find a few words to sum the whole thing up. I've got this book which is all about Aborigines and Australian art and it's called *The Dreaming*. The song was originally called 'Dreamtime', but when we found out that the other word for it was 'The Dreaming' it was so beautiful... It also seems to sum up a lot of the songs because one of the main points about that time for the Aborigines was that it was very religious and humans and animals were very closely connected. Humans were actually living in animal's bodies and that's an idea which I particularly like playing with... I have contact with a few Australians and it seems that at the moment Aboriginal art is becoming very fashionable so the young Australians are starting to take a lot more serious notice of what's happening to them."

Kate did a live performance of 'The Dreaming' on the

German TV show, *Na Sowas!* in September 1982. Originally, the plan was for the official video to be broadcast (it is unclear as to why this wasn't possible) but when everyone on set was told that the song needed to be performed live, the stage was covered in soil and polystyrene rocks. Through the magic of television, they were blown up in size and used to form the backdrop. Kate did the same dance routine as the one that features on the official video for 'The Dreaming'.

Regarding 'There Goes A Tenner', Kate said to *Keyboard* in July 1985; "That was written on the piano. I had an idea for the tune and just knocked out the chords for the first verse. The words and everything just came together. It was quite a struggle from thereon to try to keep things together. The lyrics are quite difficult on that one, because there are a lot of words in quite a short space of time. They had to be phrased right and everything. That was very difficult. Actually the writing went hand-in-hand with the Yamaha CS-80."

In an interview with *Melody Maker* in October 1982, Kate was asked; "Apart from the use of sound to conjure up very simple images you've also used list of names, like Minnie, Moony, Vicious, Buddy Holly, Sandy Denny on 'Blow Away' and Bogart, Raft and Cagney on 'There Goes A Tenner'. Are they people you particularly admire or do you just like the strong images they create?" Her response: "They are people I like. For me, Cagney is one of the greatest actors that has ever been. I just couldn't believe his acting in *White Heat*. He's always played the boy who grew up in a hard time and in a way he was only ever bad because of the things that had influenced him. He comes across as a very human person who had the potential to do something great but was always misled. In that song the idea is that everyone's amateur robbers... So it's like maybe they get a bit cocky, I dunno, I've never done a robbery, but I think that in a situation like that you'd almost try to be like the person you admire so perhaps they'd be like Cagney and George Raft. The idea was nothing like deep — it was just handy! The real challenge of that song was to make it a story but also keep it like a thirties tune."

Kate said in *Sounds* in October 1982 regarding the importance of getting into character to sing; "The song is always about something, and always from a particular viewpoint. There's normally a personality that runs along with it. Sometimes I really have to work at it to get in the right frame of mind, because it's maybe the opposite of how I'm feeling, but other times it feels almost like an extension of me, which it is, in some ways."

The video for 'There Goes A Tenner' provides a visual enhancement to the themes and ideas in the song; it is clear that the robbers don't know what they're doing and are very worried about their own incompetence. As much as Kate's music is renowned for telling a story, the video adds to this element of her work tremendously.

'Pull Out The Pin' features a persistent piano motif that rings out over the slow beat of the song. The helicopter sound was sampled from a cassette made by drummer Preston Hayman that he made in Bali. Overall, in terms of texture, the track is a busy one.

Guitarist Brian Bath said in *Uncut* in January 2012; "At one point they got everyone — kids, engineers, about fifty of us — just going 'Waaaah!' On 'Pull Out The Pin', I got this ridiculous diminished guitar lick which just went all over the place, like a Jimmy Bryant thing. Kate loved it!"

Of 'Pull Out The Pin', Kate wrote for the *Kate Bush Club* magazine in October 1982; "We sat in front of the speakers trying to focus on the picture — a green forest, humid and pulsating with life. We are looking at the Americans from the Vietnamese point of view and, almost like a camera, we start in wide shot. Right in the distance you can see the trees moving, smoke and sounds drifting our way — sounds like a radio. Closer in with the camera, and you can catch glimpses of their pink skin. We can smell them for miles with their sickly cologne, American tobacco and stale sweat. Take the camera in even closer, and we find a solitary soldier, perhaps the one I have singled out (sometimes a Vietnamese would track a soldier for days and follow him, until he eventually took him). This soldier is under a tree, dozing with a faint smile and a radio by his side. It's a small transistor radio out of which cries an electric guitar. I'd swear it was being played by Brian Bath, but how could that be, way out here on our stereo screen? I pop the silver Buddha that I wear around my neck into my mouth, securing my lips around his little metal body. I move towards the sleeping man. A helicopter soars overhead, he wakes up, and as he looks me in the eyes I relate to him as I would to a helpless stranger. Has he a family and a lady waiting for him at home, somewhere beyond the Chinese drums and the double bass that stalks like a wild cat through bamboo? The moving pictures freeze-frame and fade — someone stopped the multi-track, there's more overdubs to do."

Regarding 'Pull Out The Pin', Kate said; "I saw a programme with a cameraman on the front line in Vietnam. The Vietnamese were portrayed as being very craftful people who treated their fighting as an art. They could literally smell the Americans coming through the jungle. Their culture of Coke cans and ice creams actually made them smell. Anyway, I learnt that before the Vietnamese went into action they popped a little silver Buddha in their mouths. I thought that was quite beautiful. Grotesque beauty attracts me. Negative images are often so interesting."

She told *Sounds* in October 1982; "I didn't think I'd ever want to write about it (Vietnam) until I saw this documentary on television which moved me so much I thought I just had to."

Kate said in *Keyboard* in July 1985; "He was a brilliant cameraman and he was so well-trained a technician that he kept filming things no matter how he was feeling about it at the time. Some of the stuff he was shooting was really disturbing. Some of the Vietnamese guys would just come in and they were sort of dying in mid-air. And he'd just keep on filming."

Kate considered the story from all angles, including how the cameraman's experience had an impact on him. She said to *Zigzag* in November 1982, explaining that it was filmed "from the Vietnamese point of view, so it was very biased against the Americans. He said it really changed him, because until you live on their level like that, when it's complete survival, you don't know what it's about. He's never been the same since, because it's so devastating, people dying all the time. The way he portrayed the Vietnamese was as this really crafted, beautiful race. The Americans were these big, fat, pink, smelly things who the Vietnamese could smell coming for miles because of the tobacco and cologne. It was devastating, because you got the impression that the Americans were so heavy and awkward, and the Vietnamese were so beautiful and all getting wiped out. They wore a little silver Buddha on a chain around their neck and when they went into action they'd pop it into their mouth, so if they died they'd have Buddha on their lips. I wanted to write a song that could somehow convey the whole thing, so we set it in the jungle and had helicopters, crickets and little Balinese frogs."

Kate said of 'Suspended In Gaffa' on BBC Radio One in 1982; "Well, it's really about people that are after something that is very special to them. They've seen something that they want very badly, but they know that in order to get that they have to work very hard. And a lot of people don't want to do the work and still want the thing at the end of it. I remember when

I was at school, I was always told about purgatory as being the place that you went to and you saw a glimpse of God and then he went away and you never ever saw him again and you were in the most tremendous pain for the rest of eternity because you couldn't ever see him again. And it's a really heavy image, you know, especially for a child. And I think in many ways it's a very similar thing, trying to get that back, that thing that you really want to see again."

In *Melody Maker* in October 1982, Kate said of 'Suspended In Gaffa'; "Lyrically it's not really that dissimilar from 'Sat In Your Lap' in saying that you really want to work for something. It's playing with the idea of hell. At school I was always taught that if you went to hell you would see a glimpse of God and that was it — you never saw him again and you'd spend the rest of eternity pining to see him. In a way it was even worse if you went to purgatory because you got the glimpse of God and you would see him again but you didn't know when. So it was almost like you had to sit there until he decided to come back. I suppose for me in my work, because it's such a sped up life and so much happens to you and you analyse yourself a lot, you see the potential for perhaps getting to somewhere very special on an artistic or a spiritual level and that excites me a lot. And it's the idea of working towards that and perhaps one day, when you're ready for that change, it's like entering a different level of existence, where everything goes slow-mo — it's almost like a religious experience. That's basically what the song's about... I think I very much believe in the forces and energies that humans and other things which are alive can create. I do feel that what you give out sincerely then karmically you should get it back... I think it's also about the way you try to work for something and you end up finding you've been working away from it rather than towards it. It's really about the whole frustration of having to wait for things — the fact that you can't do what you want to do now, you have to work towards it and maybe, only maybe, in five years you'll get what you're after. For me there are so many things I do which I don't want to — the mechanics of the industry — but I hope that through them I can get what I really want. You have to realise that, say, you can't just be an artist and not promote. If you're not a salesman for your work the likelihood is that people won't realise that it's there and eventually you'll stop yourself from being able to make something else. There's no doubt about it that every album I make is really dependant on the money I made from the last one."

When talking to *New Musical Express* the same month she added; "'Suspended In Gaffa' is reasonably autobiographical, which most of my songs aren't. It's about seeing something that you want — on any level — and not being able to get that thing unless you work hard and in the right way towards it. When I do that I become aware of so many obstacles, and then I want the thing without the work. And then when you achieve it you enter a different level — everything will slightly change. It's like going into a time warp which otherwise wouldn't have existed. Oh yes, quite a few people have surmised that from listening to the song. But when you explain it like this it doesn't sound like anything. The idea is much more valuable within the song than it is in my telling you about it. When you analyse it, it seems silly."

'Suspended In Gaffa' has an almost pantomime-like quality to it. It is a waltz punctuated with an upbeat staccato with moments of apparent cynicism. Throughout the song, it sounds very much like Kate is singing from the back of her throat — almost as if she is gulping her way through the lyrics. This would certainly explain why she expressed concerns about the technicalities of singing the song.

Kate wrote for the *Kate Bush Club* magazine in October

1982; "Whenever I've sung this song I've hoped that my breath would hold out for the first few phrases, as there is no gap to breathe in. When I wrote this track the words came at the same time, and this is one of the few songs where the lyrics were complete at such an early stage. The idea of the song is that of being given a glimpse of "God" — something that we dearly want — but being told that unless we work for it, we will never see it again, and even then, we might not be worthy of it. Of course, everybody wants the reward without the toil, so people try to find a way out of the hard work, still hoping to claim the prize, but such is not the case. The choruses are meant to express the feeling of entering timelessness as you become ready for the experience, but only when you are ready."

In *Company* in January 1982, Kate was quoted as referring to her voice as her "precious instrument — it can be affected by almost anything — my nerves, my mood, even the weather."

By the time it came to making *The Dreaming*, Kate's voice had been on quite the journey. She said of her singing style in a TV interview on *Saturday Superstore* in October 1982; "I think that's something that grew over the years, because when I first started singing I had a very untoneful voice. I mean I could sing in tune, but there was no quality to my voice at all. And over the years, the more I kept singing the more it started changing and growing."

She told *Zigzag* in November 1982; "This is the first time that I actually enjoy listening to my voice. It's a big breakthrough. Though *Never For Ever* was getting there, it was really compromise all the way, because I couldn't do any better at the time. I think it's the vocal chords as you get older. They do something. I can actually put some balls into my voice for the first time. It's exciting!"

From humble beginnings... When asked if she'd had singing lessons, Kate said on BBC Radio One in 1982; "Yes

I did actually with a really lovely man called Mr Farrell. And I used to go there for half an hour, once a week. And I'd sit and play him my latest song, and then we'd do some breathing exercises and a couple of songs that were standards and I'd go away. And what was really great about it was that he gave me a tremendous amount of confidence in my voice, which I really didn't have much of."

Regarding her vocal technique, Kate said; "I've stretched the pitch range over the years. What I used to do in my earlier performing was to go for notes higher than I could reach easily in the song, so by the time I'd written the song and played it for a good few days, I could actually reach those notes. By making my writing more acrobatic than I was, I was stretching myself to it. It's something that's grown over the years. Definitely my voice has got stronger in the last two years, because on *The Dreaming* I was so aware of the difference in my voice. Not only is it much stronger, but it is also more controlled. It has been frustrating for me in the past because my voice has never sounded the way I wanted it to, and so whenever I was listening to the albums it was unbearable for me. It was not just the weakness, but the style of it. I've always tried to get my voice the way it's starting to be now. Because the songs always controlled me, they were always tending to be in a higher range. It sounds strange, but I think that when you write songs, very often you don't have control of them. You can guide them, but they have their own life force, really. My use of decorative notes probably comes from Irish music. My mother's Irish, and in my childhood my brothers were very into traditional music and we could hear it in the house all the time. The airs and inflections are beautiful, and I love Irish singing. On 'Night Of The Swallow' Liam O'Flynn plays the uilleann pipes and the penny whistle, to give the track an Irish flavour. I think my use of thirds is because in a lot of songs there are times when I want it to sound like someone actually talking rather than singing. There are things that you say that often people don't put into songs, and I quite like to use those lines. Quite often when people speak they naturally use the 'third-to-root' pitch-change in their voices — little tension marks that take it up a couple of tones... I do feel that every song comes from a different person, really, so this is one way of making something different about it. I like to "create" voices. I've been trying this over the years. I often find that I do "word painting" without realising, and my singing/speech style probably comes from the Irish influence again. Sometimes I don't think the words are important, and I'll just use sound shapes, which establish the mood. The lyrics of the lead vocal are awfully important to me, while the backing vocals are very often just trying to create a picture, as in *The Dreaming*."

Kate also spoke about other effects; "I hardly ever use the Vocoder — only once for a tiny effect on 'Babooshka' to make the drum sound like the title. We've been experimenting a lot with effects units — particularly the flanger, to get different textures with the voices. In several of the songs there are at least four or five layers of voices. In order to have them not sounding like one clump, we've had to try and separate them by treating them and placing them carefully in the stereo field. Some have more reverb or more echo than others, too."

The vocals on 'Leave It Open' are heavily processed. Just like Queen's 'We Will Rock You', the rhythm section is clever because it has an almost tribal feel to it that is immensely memorable. Throughout the track, Kate often places a vocal emphasis on the downbeats. Even the piano is used as a percussive instrument in this song whereby the chords are stabbed at to an extent that they emphasise what is going on with the drums. The character of the whole song feels urgent and confrontational.

Kate said in *New Musical Express* in October 1982; "I don't sit down and try to express mystery. I worry that I try too hard to create spontaneity. I can be singing a song of a calm person who suddenly becomes aggressive, and I try and reflect that vocally. Different ideas come across in different accents... 'Leave It Open' is the idea of human beings being like cups — like receptive vessels. We open and shut ourselves at different times. It's very easy to let your ego go "nag nag nag" when you should shut it. Or when you're very narrow-minded and you should be open. Finally you should be able to control your levels of receptivity to a productive end."

Of 'Leave It Open', Kate wrote for the *Kate Bush Club* magazine in October 1982, "Like cups, we are filled up and emptied with feelings, emotions — vessels breathing in, breathing out. This song is about being open and shut to stimuli at the right times. Often we have closed minds and open mouths when perhaps we should have open minds and shut mouths. This was the first demo to be recorded, and we used a Revox and the few effects such as a guitar chorus pedal and an analogue delay system. We tried to give the track an Eastern flavour and the finished demo certainly had a distinctive mood. There are lots of different vocal parts, each portraying a separate character and therefore each demanding an individual sound. When a lot of vocals are being used in contrast rather than "as one", more emphasis has to go on distinguishing between the different voices, especially if the vocals are coming from one person. To help the separation we used the effects we had. When we mastered the track, a lot more electronic effects and different kinds of echoes were used, helping to place the vocals and give a greater sense of perspective."

'Night Of The Swallow' is full of fascinating contrasts. It moves between Irish folk music and a very spacious piano part. In response to the question of "How did you get involved with

(Irish folk band) Planxty?" Kate replied on BBC Radio One in 1982; "Well, I've been a fan of theirs as well. Really, my brother Jay (Kate's eldest brother, John Carder Bush) played me some albums of theirs and ever since I've been hooked. I wrote the song and it just seemed perfect for them to work on. So I rang a guy called Bill Whelan, who's the keyboard player, and he was really interested in it and said he'd get the guys together, but over in Ireland. So I had to fly over there for the day and we put them on tape. And Bill wrote this fantastic arrangement, which he originally played to me there on the phone, it was fantastic!"

When asked whether the track featuring Planxty was inspired by her own Irish roots, Kate replied in an interview with BBC Radio Two in September 1982; "Yes, very much so, because my mother is Irish and when I was very little the music in the house was Irish traditional music. And I think I've always loved it... When I wrote the song I felt straight away that the choruses were just waiting for something like an Irish band and it was just a matter of getting in touch with the people from Planxty and seeing if they were willing to do it. And I managed to contact a man called Bill Whelan, who's the keyboard player in Planxty, and he arranged the whole passage in the choruses. And it's really beautiful, I think it's changed the song a great deal, and definitely for the better."

Regarding working with Planxty on 'Night Of The Swallow', Kate said in *Zigzag* in November 1982; "They were incredible: the energy and attitude towards recording music. We worked from five in the afternoon till eight the next morning, then went straight to the airport. The whole idea of the song was that the choruses were this guy flying off. He's a pilot who's been offered a load of money if he doesn't ask any questions. He really wants to do it, for the challenge as well, but his wife is really against it because she feels he's going to get caught. The verses are her saying 'Don't do it!' and the choruses are him saying 'Look, I can do it, I can fly like a swallow'."

In October 1982 in *Melody Maker*, Kate said of 'Night Of The Swallow'; "Unfortunately a lot of men do begin to feel very trapped in their relationships and I think, in some situations, it is because the female is so scared, perhaps of her insecurity, that she needs to hang onto him completely. In this song she wants to control him and because he wants to do something that she doesn't want him to, she feels that he is going away. It's almost on a parallel with the mother and son relationship where there is the same female feeling of not wanting the young child to move away from the nest. Of course, from the guy's point of view, because she doesn't want him to go, the urge to go is even stronger. For him, it's not so much a job as a challenge; a chance to do something risky and exciting. But although that woman's very much a stereotype I think she still exists today."

Writing for the *Kate Bush Club* magazine in October 1982 she explained; "Ever since I heard my first Irish pipe music it has been under my skin, and every time I hear the pipes, it's like someone tossing a stone in my emotional well, sending ripples down my spine. I've wanted to work with Irish music for years, but my writing has never really given me the opportunity of doing so until now. As soon as the song was written, I felt that a ceilidh band would be perfect for the choruses. The verses are about a lady who's trying to keep her man from accepting what seems to be an illegal job. He is a pilot and has been hired to fly some people into another country. No questions are to be asked, and she gets a bad feeling from the situation. But for him, the challenge is almost more exciting than the job itself, and he wants to fly away. As the fiddles, pipes and whistles start up in the choruses, he is explaining how it will be all right. He'll hide the plane high up in the clouds on a night with no moon, and he'll swoop over the water like a swallow. Bill Whelan is the keyboard player with Planxty, and ever since Jay played me an album of theirs I have been a fan. I rang Bill and he tuned into the idea of the arrangement straight away. We sent him a cassette, and a few days later he phoned the studio and said, 'Would you like to hear the arrangement I've written?' I said I'd love to, but how? 'Well, Liam is with me now, and we could play it over the phone.' I thought how wonderful he was, and I heard him put down the phone and walk away. The cassette player started up. As the chorus began, so did this beautiful music — through the wonder of telephones it was coming live from Ireland, and it was very moving. We arranged that I would travel to Ireland with Jay and the multi-track tape, and that we would record in Windmill Lane Studios, Dublin. As the choruses began to grow, the evening drew on and the glasses of Guinness, slowly dropping in level, became like sand glasses to tell the passing of time. We missed our plane and worked through the night. By eight o'clock the next morning we were driving to the airport to return to London. I had a very precious tape tucked under my arm, and just as we were stepping onto the plane, I looked up into the sky and there were three swallows diving and chasing the flies."

'Night Of The Swallow' offers something more melodic than the other tracks on the album, as does 'All The Love' — both songs are on the more gentle side; brooding ballads with an enchanting atmosphere that are more reminiscent of Kate's softer musical style. They both create a false sense of security prior to the volatile nature of 'Get Out Of My House' following 'Houdini'.

Overall, the contemporary feel to *The Dreaming* is plausibly reflective of the music that Kate was most engaged with listening to at the time. She said on BBC Radio Two in September 1982; "I think classical music is very inspirational. Again, because it's normally quite visual, you close your eyes and wonderful landscapes start happening. So I'm sure it has been very inspirational but I listen to a lot more contemporary stuff now."

Influences aside though, Kate's aspirations to get emotions across in her music were just as present on *The Dreaming* as any of her other albums. She said in the same interview; "I think the main aim is to get some kind of emotional impact across, and hopefully it's the emotional situation that goes with the subject matter of the song."

Of 'All The Love' Kate wrote for the *Kate Bush Club* magazine in October 1982; "Although we are often surrounded by people and friends, we are all ultimately alone, and I feel sure everyone feels lonely at some time in their life. I wanted to write about feeling alone, and how having to hide emotions away or being too scared to show love can lead to being lonely as well. There are just some times when you can't cope and you just don't feel you can talk to anyone. I go and find a bathroom, a toilet or an empty room just to sit and let it out and try to put it all together in my mind. Then I go back and face it all again. I think it's sad how we forget to tell people we love that we do love them. Often we think about these things when it's too late or when an extreme situation forces us to show those little things we're normally too shy or too lazy to reveal. One of the ideas for the song sparked when I came home from the studio late one night. I was using an answering machine to take the day's messages and it had been going wrong a lot, gradually growing worse with time. It would speed people's voices up beyond recognition, and I just used to hope they would ring back again one day at normal speed. This particular night, I started to play back the tape, and the machine had neatly edited half a dozen messages together to leave 'Goodbye', 'See you!', 'Cheers', 'See you soon' — It was a strange thing to sit and listen to your friends ringing up apparently just to say goodbye. I had several cassettes of people's messages all ending with authentic farewells, and by copying them onto a quarter inch tape and re-arranging the order, we managed to synchronise the "callers" with the last verse of the song. There are still quite a few of my friends who have not heard the album or who have not recognised themselves and are still wondering how they managed to appear in the album credits when they didn't even set foot into the studio."

Kate told *Melody Maker*; "Whenever I've experienced a relationship, or the people around me have, it's always ended up being incredibly complicated because that's the way human beings are. Nothing is simple, it always ends up being something else or dying and that's what I find so interesting — the drive behind human beings and the way they get screwed up."

The melancholic verse/chorus sections in 'All The Love' convey the themes of the song very effectively. Kate said in *Zigzag* in November 1982; "Some of them are definitely parts of me. I think 'All The Love' definitely says something — not necessarily the negative side of me but the self-pitying side. The way you look at human beings and yourself, and think we're just a heap of shit. If we weren't so scared of saying what we meant, it would be so much better. All the times you didn't say things to people, either because of pride, or rejection fears — that sort of thing. That may not be an example of my own life, but I felt it nearly happening. It's just a terrible feeling, the thought of people having gone without the right amount of feedback. I think that really fucks people up. There are loads of people who spend all day saying, 'What do you think?' I get an awful lot of feedback; even if it's negative it's better than nothing."

Amongst the emotion, was technology. Kate explained to *Electronics & Music Maker* in October 1982; "We have used delay machines for this on a couple of tracks, and added a very slight harmoniser effect, as well as sometimes very tight double tracking. It really does depend on the song, and how strong the lead vocal needs to be. For a more delicate song it would be wrong to put a heavy harmoniser on it — it would sound so affected. We've also been using an awful lot of compression on the new album — with nearly everything, in fact. It's interesting, the kind of dynamics you can actually create, which is what I really never understood before. Especially with voices — as you start compressing them more and more, so many different levels start coming through on it — the breath particularly. And for me, that's as important as the words: it's the space in between… (on 'All The Love') it's the idea of using the breath as a voice. There was another backing vocal sung by our engineer, and it's fantastic, because in the gaps there are these huge passages of him going 'haahuuh!' where you can feel the breath moving past."

In an interview with BBC Radio One in 1982, Kate said; "There's a wonderful fretless bass player from Germany called Eberhard Weber who I think I've mentioned to you before… I'm a very big fan of his. And he played on the track 'Houdini' which was wonderful. And Dave Gilmour came in as well and did some vocals on one of the tracks."

She told *New Musical Express*; "I realise how lucky I am. I realised, making *The Dreaming*, when I was able to get Eberhard Weber to play on one track, that I was so lucky because people you like and respect will want to work with you."

Kate said on BBC Radio Two in September 1982; "Houdini, I think most people know him for being the escapologist, the man who's wriggling around in a sack on the pavement. But I started finding out about a side of his life that seemed more interesting, for me, where he spent a lot of years actually going around to mediums and séances, exposing the fact that they were frauds. He'd try to contact his mother when she died and he just met fraud after fraud and they were after his money and

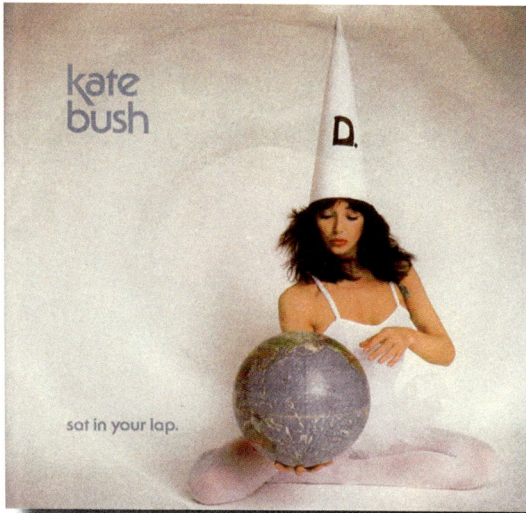

Over a year before the album appeared 'Sat In Your Lap' was released as a single. The same picture sleeve was used globally but — one for collectors — there were label variations.

UK

Australia

Brazil

Unlike Kate's debut album, *The Dreaming* wasn't released with different sleeve designs around the world although the Japanese version had the usual obi strip.

Australia

Canada

Greece

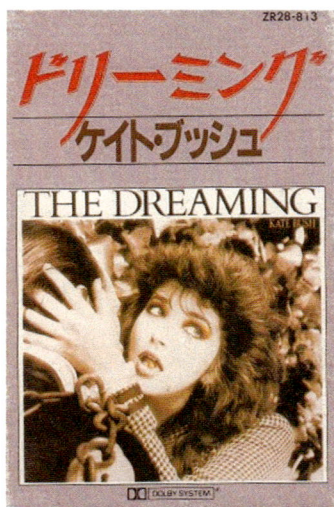

Japan

At least there was a bit of variation with the cassette versions for the avid collectors amongst Kate's fan base, as these examples show.

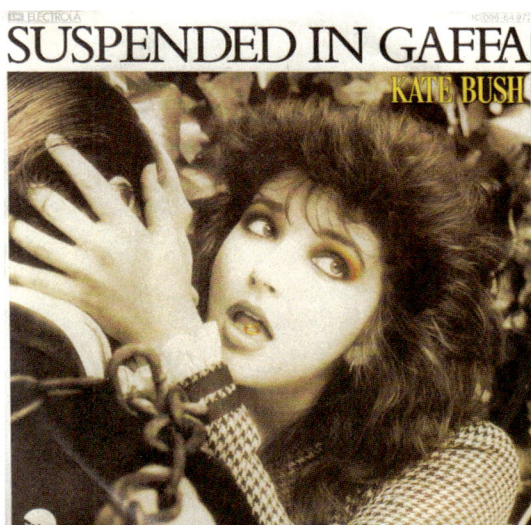

Despite the album being Kate's least commercial release at the time, EMI still tried to push singles from it. 'Suspended In Gaffa' wasn't released in the UK but it was put out in Australia and across Europe.

'The Dreaming' single appropriately used Aboriginal art on the picture sleeve.

'There Goes A Tenner' was only released as a single in the British Isles.

Since the album was released on CD, EMI Japan has gone into overdrive, re-issuing the album at alarming regularity, each time with a different obi strip.

UK

A custom label design was used in most countries but some such as Ireland used a standard EMI design.

as far he was concerned they were just making people very unhappy just in order to get money. So he spent years just going 'round to these places, and revealing the wires and revealing the technicalities and all this sort of thing. But between him and his wife they made a code and it was very strange because they made this so that if perhaps one of them ever died and the other tried to contact them through a medium or a séance, that they would know that it was really them and not a fraud. And when Houdini died his wife did actually start going around to the mediums and the séances, more or less what he had done when he had been alive. And the same thing for years, she just came across so many fakes and people that really were not true mediums at all. Until one day she had a phone call from a man who said that Houdini had come through to him. So she went to see him, and he gave her the code that only Houdini and her had known and as far as she was concerned he had made contact with her. It is really all about her and him and how very much in love they were and how terrible it was for her when he died, but that they did make contact again. So it's all about that special moment."

Kate went above and beyond in researching the subject matter of the song. She told *Zigzag* in November 1982; "It's such a beautiful image: for this guy, who'd been escaping all his life, to escape death and come back to her. But I didn't know if he had come back, because the other stories said he hadn't, so I rang up *Psychic News*, and this nice lady got all these papers from the 1920s and read me this apparently official declaration from Mrs Houdini that this had happened. I feel that they were terribly in love because of the whole story. She was saving his life every time. It's such a great story, I couldn't resist it."

On BBC Radio Two in September 1982, in response to the question of "Houdini's wife in that particular track was, as it were, possessed, there was quite a lot of distortion. How did you achieve that effect?" Kate said, "The idea is that it's as she's watching him go off into his tank of water for the last time, and it's the idea that she is this sort of possessed demon that's terrified of him going. And I drank about a pint of milk before I did the vocal and ate like two bars of chocolate. And the great thing about those sort of foods is it really creates a lot of mucus and normally that's the last thing you want when you sing, you normally want a very pure voice, but I wanted to get all that sort of spit and gravel in the throat. So I worked on bringing the gravel out and as I sung we sped the track up a bit so that when it was played back the voice would just be slightly deeper, just have slightly more weight in it."

For the *Kate Bush Club* magazine Kate wrote; "His mother had died, and in trying to make contact through such spiritual people, he realised how much pain was being inflicted on people already in sorrow, people who would part with money just for the chance of a few words from a past loved one. I feel he must have believed in the possibility of contact after death, and perhaps in his own way, by weeding out the frauds, he hoped to find just one that could not be proven to be a fake… It is such a beautiful and strange story that I thought I had very little to do, other than tell it like it was. But in fact it proved to be the most difficult lyric of all the songs and the most emotionally demanding. I was so aware of trying to do justice to the beauty of the subject, and trying to understand what it must have been like to have been in love with such an extraordinary man, and to have been loved by him. I worked for two or three nights just to find one line that was right. There were so many alternatives, but only a few were right for the song. Gradually it grew and began to piece together, and I found myself wrapped up in the feelings of the song — almost pining for Houdini. Singing the lead vocal was a matter of conjuring up that feeling again and as the clock whirrs and the song flashes back in time to when she watched him through the glass, he's on the other side under water, and she hangs on to his every breath. We both wait."

In *Zigzag* in November 1982, it was mentioned by the interviewer that Kate was considering 'Houdini' for release as a single but was reluctant about it. She was quoted on the matter; "I feel under pressure to go with the obvious one." As for what she may have felt was the obvious choice, nothing else was mentioned.

'Get Out Of My House' is certainly a brutal way to end an album. With a pounding drumbeat and an vicious lead guitar part, it is a volatile track full of repetitive chord changes. The song stays mostly in common time but an almost dizzying effect is achieved by the moments in which it goes into 2/4 time. Kate told *Zigzag* in November 1982; "It's meant to be a bit scary. It's just the idea of someone being in this place and there's something else there — you don't know what it is. The track kept changing in the studio. This is something that's never happened before on an album. That one was maybe half the length it is now. The guitarist got this really nice riff going, and I got this idea of two voices — a person in the house, trying to get away from this thing, but it's still there. So in order to get away, they change their form — first into a bird trying to fly away from it. The thing can change as well, so that changes into this wind, and starts blowing all icy. The idea is to turn around and face it. You've got this image of something turning round and going 'Aah!' just to try and scare it away."

She said to *Company* in January 1982; "It's all about the human as a house. The idea is that as more experiences actually get to you, you start learning how to defend yourself from them. The human can be seen as a house where you start putting up shutters at the windows and locking the doors — not letting in certain things. I think a lot of people are like this — they don't hear what they don't want to hear, don't see what they don't want to see. It is like a house, where the windows are the eyes and the ears, and you don't let people in. That's sad because as they grow older people should open up more. But they do the opposite because, I suppose, they do get bruised and cluttered. Which brings me back to myself — yes, I have had to decide what I will let in and what I'll have to exclude."

She told *Melody Maker* in 1982; "The idea with that song is that the house is actually a human being who's been hurt and he's just locking all the doors and not letting anyone in. The person is so determined not to let anyone in that one of his personalities is a concierge who sits in the door, and says 'you're not coming in here' — like a real mamma."

As ever, 'Get Out Of My House' certainly wasn't the first of Kate's songs to be inspired by literature. In September 1982 on BBC Radio Two, she said of her ideas; "They're very often ideas that come out of other people's creations. Films and books are very much big inspirations to me. For instance, there's a track on this album that really, the whole atmosphere was inspired by *The Shining*. I read the book and it was such an incredibly strong atmosphere, very creepy, very haunted, and I used it to set a song using the same atmosphere, but instead of it being a hotel, it is like a house, which is also a human being; just playing with the feelings that I got when I read the book and trying to put that same kind and strangeness into the song."

Kate wrote for the *Kate Bush Club* magazine in October 1982; "*The Shining* is the only book I've read that has frightened me. While reading it I swamped around in its snowy imagery and avoided visiting certain floors of the big, cold hotel, empty for the winter. As in *Alien*, the central characters are isolated, miles (or light years) away from anyone or anything, but there is something in the place with them. They're not sure what, but it isn't very nice. The setting for this song continues the theme — the house which is really a human being, has been shut up — locked and bolted, to stop any outside forces from entering. The person has been hurt and has decided to keep everybody out. They plant a "concierge" at the front door to stop any determined callers from passing, but the thing has got into the house upstairs. It's descending in the lift, and now it approaches the door of the room that you're hiding in. You're cornered, there's no way out, so you turn into a bird and fly away, but the thing changes shape, too. You change, it changes; you can't escape, so you turn around and face it, scare it away."

In *Melody Maker* Kate said; "Whenever I do read, it really sparks things off in me. The last book I read was *The Shining* and it just blew me away, it was absolutely brilliant, and that definitely inspired 'Get Out Of My House' because the atmosphere of the book is so strong."

Of course, the subject matters that influenced Kate's writing were always broad. She said on BBC Radio Two in September 1982; "I think the state of the world influences me a lot, I think it does every writer... I think I'm more concerned with the psychological side of human beings. I am a romanticist as well. But I think I'm very interested in the way that people's brains work, they're very different from each other sometimes."

The cover art on *The Dreaming* features autumnal shades — sepia. Kate is clasping the head of a man in chains and in her mouth is a tiny gold key. She was quoted in *Melody Maker* in October 1982; "The idea of that image and the phrase on the back of the album, 'with a kiss I'd pass the key', is very much connected to the song 'Houdini.' That song is taken from Mrs Houdini's point of view because she spent a lot of time working with him and helping with his tricks. One of the ways she would help was to give him a parting kiss, just as he was off into his water tank or whatever, and as she kissed him she'd pass a tiny little key which he would then use later to unlock the padlocks. I thought it was both a very romantic and a very sad image because, by passing that key, she is keeping him alive — she's actually giving him the key back into life."

The amount of time spent on making *The Dreaming* wasn't necessarily intentional as Kate explained to *Sounds* in October 1982; "I find that a lot of things I do now take so much longer than I thought they would… In so many cases you need to be in the studio to get the sounds, and it can maybe take a couple of days just to get one idea across. Sometimes you wonder if you should just leave them."

The length and expense of the studio time that it took to finish *The Dreaming* was such that EMI expressed doubts over how the album would pay off in proportion to those factors. Thereafter, Kate made the decision to build her own studio in order that she could spend as much time as she liked working in it without having to worry about bookings, schedules and related overheads. A good decision as Kate explained in *Electronics & Music Maker* in October 1982; "Normally I've recorded between Air and Abbey Road Studios, but this time I seemed to make the album at studios where I had to grab time between other major artists, because I wanted particular facilities. We worked at the Townhouse, Abbey Road, Odyssey Studios, and did the digital mix at Advision Studios with Paul Hardiman using the Sony machine. The final recording wasn't digital, even though I would prefer to do it that way. Editing with the digital recorder did seem to be difficult — some things were quicker, but others were easily three times as long."

When asked if her music required a lot of editing, Kate was quoted in the same feature; "It really did this time, especially when you've got mixes that are very complicated and demanding. We'd get the whole mix and there'd be one little bit that wasn't quite right, or an echo plate would distort on us. Then we'd just have to edit that in. Having got the whole field right, it seems crazy to do a whole track again, so we prefer to do spot edits."

It wasn't just the editing that was time consuming. Kate said; "First we do all the backing tracks in one go, and then we'd work on it in layers until we'd got all the other musicians out of the way, so then I can really concentrate on my own stuff. It took weeks to do the vocals, especially because we were having to find the right effects and ambience for each voice. Then on top of that came the Fairlight... I did as much work on the Fairlight at home as I could, but it got very difficult because I was usually in the studio all day, and when I got back at night there were tapes of that day's stuff that I would listen to in order to decide what to go on to the next day. So in fact I wasn't really getting much time, and when I could, I'd tend to do the Fairlight in studio meal breaks in the control room... I suppose I could have done tracks like 'The Dreaming' with a large amount of Fairlight, but it does lack a little top for some sounds, and there are some things, like loops, that can be tricky to do. I ended up using three or four of the presets available on the Fairlight's menu, while most of the others were sampled. What we tended to do was try samples at home, although they would often be too noisy to use, so we'd then do them again in the studio. I have to be honest about the instrument — I really only have a working knowledge, and everything I want to do I can. I love the sampling facility, it's one of the best things — being able to put your own sounds in and then play around with them. Features like the reverse play are useful too. There's loads I can't do yet, I'm sure, but I'm taking it step by step... It does work so well for me. As an educational instrument, too, it's fantastic. Initially, I thought a lot about buying one because it was so much money. When I started this album I did try hiring one in, but it was costing me so much, and I knew that to do everything I wanted I'd need it more or less all the time, so I decided to buy it, and haven't regretted it once. I'm also interested in the new rhythm facilities now available."

After *The Dreaming*, although the next album would be a long time in gestation, it was ultimately the direction that would see Kate return to making a style of music that was considered by many to be more commercial.

Laugh? I could have Di-ed

Prince's Trust Royal Gala
Dominion

FOUR WEEKS of us they/aren't they speculation about who was actually going to play this exclusive charity do didn't apparently help to sell tickets to the gilt-trust.

The remainder, Lord preserve us, had to be sold to the public at large and a good thing too. Instead of party executives and self-absorbed 'celebrities', it was peopled mostly by metal towers and that rather than the presence of HRH, is what flavoured the atmosphere.

That, and the fact of having a selection of the very best of British musicians under one roof made it quite a unique occasion.

Madness kicked off with a jaunty version of the national anthem, and weren't all that inspiring. HRH didn't think so either and spent the time pacing at the TV monitor, scratching his left ear, and smiling wanly.

Maybe he was trying to remember the carefully rehearsed speech he was going to deliver about the wilchess of the Trust Fund music competition, blue-wile reggae outfit Unity, who, despite the towering inference told in their day, were quite acceptable. Who's to bet that they won't be allowed to slip back into obscurity?

Formalities over, we were refreshed by the all too brief appearance of Joan Armatrading and, you know, it gives me a kick still to me an audience held captive by the bass power of one guitar and the impact of a voice. The full with techno-rock and electro-loop, gizmos wibble in simplicity anytime. 'Love Is Trouble' was around with more pathos than can ever be reproduced on vinyl.

And from the sublime to . . .? Britain's most famous fish farmer bounced to him a chancer and tights with a bulge that'd put Nureyev to shame?

Jethro Tull of course, and for ten minutes we were transported to the expanses of the Wembley Arena with flash lighting, the whole works and Ian Anderson weaving into the stage like a drunken morris dancer. Maybe he imagined he was dodging snipers. I heard he'd arrived early afternoon to painstakingly check out the stage for suspect devices although the protectiveness of the previous day had us all covertly looking under our seats.

Phil Collins was guesting on the percussion hot-seat which he then seceded to render a disappointingly dull version of 'In The Air Tonight'. We were then 'entertained' by the Masai Dance Company, muscular black guys in shorts with an embarrassingly impo-ordinated routine – in obvious filler.

But the climax was worth the wait. To see Townshend . . . Uni, Kern, Collins, Bronton, Plant and Bush onstage at once was third degree culture shock! Everyone did their party piece, the highlights being a superbly textured version of 'No Regrets' with Townshend adding backing vocals, a nostalgic blast from Brooker as is with 'Whiter Shade of Pale' and an intriguingly poignant song from Townshend seeing his fortune guitar for piano. Shamefully, I've no idea of its origin but I listened to find them out.

Kate Bush made a brief but well received appearance, especially well-received when her straps broke and she had to make a dressings exit curtsying modestly to her bosom! And then Robert Plant joined the party, and discrimination gave way to sheer disbelief.

I mean, see Mick Karn shuffling limb pirouettes around Robert Plant and Pete Townshend does little to imbue you with a great sense of reality!

The grand finale was a grossly top-heavy version of 'Gonna Take You Higher' with Masai Dancers and pelvic thrusts in wild abundance. Even HRH seemed to be in the groove! And the evening wasn't over, hosted by Kid Jensen's cloying presence in being MC.

HELEN FITZGERALD

KATE BUSH seen moments before the strain proved too much: Robert Plant thrusts away regardless

Chapter Three

A Legacy

*T*he *Dreaming* seemed to signify where Kate Bush wanted to be with her work at the time. As she explained in *New Musical Express* in October 1982; "*The Dreaming* is very different from my first two records. Each time I do an LP it feels like the last one was years and years before. The essence of what I'm playing has been there from the start — it's just that the expression has been changing. What I'm doing now is what I was trying to do four years ago."

At the time of its release, *The Dreaming* was met with a mixed reception. Many were frustrated that it wasn't accessible. It was reviewed in *Record Mirror* in September 1982; "Quaint, admirable, unclassified, Kate Bush goes her own sweet way… A little outside quality control might not have gone amiss… Growing technically but showing few signs of really maturing in her work."

On Radio One's *Roundtable*, Jonathan King spoke highly of *The Dreaming*, as did Ian Gillan. (While we're on the subject of Deep Purple, Jimmy Bain who had played in Ritchie Blackmore's Rainbow played bass on *The Dreaming* on 'Sat In Your Lap', 'Leave It Open' and 'Get Out Of My House').

Under the heading of "A Brand Of Make-Believe", journalist Rose Rouse reviewed *The Dreaming* in *Sounds* in September 1982; "Kate Bush does provoke reaction. You can't wash her down with a glass of vermouth while posing on the patio. The world suddenly becomes black and white. She's not a walk-over or something to toss over your shoulder. I'm a blank sheet. Three hearings later, I feel sick. My stomach has turned. My first reaction was revulsion at the over-production. This is Ms Bush's utopia. She has realised her fantasy in the studio. It reminds me of how I felt after seeing *All That Jazz* where Bob Fosse indulges in a director's orgy. Here, Kate Bush unleashes every special effect available in sound engineering. It's a barrage with no real roughage. My second reaction was confusion. I felt swamped by Ms Bush's constant flight to the symbolic and esoteric. She takes pathos and rams it against a thick wall of sickly strings. I can't escape. Every song becomes an epic endeavour — a *Ben Hur* with shades of *Don Giovanni*. My third reaction was shock. I read the lyric sheet. I'm sitting there under the impression that Ms Bush is floating on a terminal cloud nine when I stumble across some real thoughts. 'The Dreaming' deals with the abuse and wiping out of the aborigines by the white man. Beneath the grandiose veneer lies a hard core. You would never dream it but there's more. 'Pull Out The Pin' is about the nobility of the Vietnamese in war. They put their silver Buddhas in their mouths before they went into action. It's a worthy theme but a horribly romantic treatment and you can hear Bush sighing at the aesthetic beauty of it all. My fourth reaction is depression. After the positive ideas of the first side in 'Leave It Open', 'Sat In Your Lap' and 'There Goes A Tenner' comes a sentimental fog. The melodrama is hammed up to the hilt. Ms Bush falls easily into the maudlin mood with those prize tearjerkers 'All The Love' and 'Houdini'. On reflection after initial reactions, I can't help admiring her eccentric spirit and her *voice*. She has to be praised for bringing in Rolf Harris on his didgeridoo, Percy Edwards with his animal noises, an Irish jig band and a choirboy. Her sense of adventure is evidently intact but she crammed in too much. I'm drowning in a sea of vocal overdubs. My taste buds have been over-stimulated. It took a year, five studios and five engineers to make this record. It shows."

A few weeks after the above review was printed in *Sounds*, two fans, Sam Johnson and Bill Blackstone, responded to it via the letters page: "Rose Rouse does provoke reaction. Her review of Kate Bush's *The Dreaming* cannot readily be washed down by a cup of coffee as one relaxes in the study bedroom. Our first reaction was of despair. Why is it that *Sounds* reviewers so often greet the most inventive rock artists of the day with little more than distain and pretentious verbiage? Kate Bush's imaginative, progressive talent can only be compared with the likes of Gabriel and not in advancing the frontiers of rock music, while drawing heavily on its ethnic roots. In fact we would congratulate the reviewer of the latest Peter Gabriel album for showing (on the very same page) an awareness, albeit limited and somewhat confused, of its achievement. Ms Rouse seems to react to the creativity and variety of *The Dreaming* with mere incomprehension and to mistake compassion and sensitivity for the 'hamming and ramming' of 'melodrama' and 'sentimentality'. Our second reaction was of pity, and we ask does Miss Rouse relish the reduction of music to its most banal and base? The problems of her digestive system are no doubt the result of the paucity of inventiveness of today's rock music. Against this background, Miss Bush's offerings are a rare feast of what the best-loved musical talents and sound engineering can produce. It took small appreciation of inventive rock music and perhaps only five minutes of prejudice to write the review. It showed."

It was considered by *Zigzag* that, "*The Dreaming* was a brave step. Not easy enough for the radio so it stiffed. But Kate stands by it as a necessary trailer for the breadth and progress of her strange new album. She can be a popstar or go on and break ground way beyond the Radio One rhino enclosure where feeding time is all glossy white soul and those covers. *The Dreaming* can't even be spotted in the hills. It pulses with new shapes and guises, voices crawl over your ears and gnaw the brain like beautiful maggots. The drums are enormous, the spaces cavernous. Few songs have an actual chorus but each has its own atmosphere and theme, from a macabre look at Vietnam to pure horror. Life and death. I was bowled over by the new depth and range in Kate's voice. The new deep one on *The Dreaming* contrasting with the airy familiar. A cracked rasp slicing through 'Houdini', defiant screams frazzling 'Pull Out The Pin' while a nest of demons burst out of the stomach on 'Get Out Of My House'. Backwards and beyond 'Leave It Open'."

In actual fact, all ten songs on *The Dreaming* follow various kinds of traditional verse-chorus-bridge structures but it is interesting to observe that not everyone who listened to the album noticed that. And it's completely understandable too; the songs aren't always instantly memorable because they very often lack a hook melody. On such basis, they can easily go over the listener's head. Even Kate herself advocated that *The Dreaming* required more than one listen for someone to really be able to get into it. "I know where all the choruses are because they're so obvious to me… It's quite likely too, that people say they can't dance to my music at parties or discos, but of course, I can dance to it, so it doesn't bother me."

It was considered in *Melody Maker* in October 1982; "To some people, Kate Bush has almost ceased to exist. Usurped on the bedroom walls by young upstarts like Clare Grogan and Kim Wilde, she is now a much more private lady who rarely goes out and seems quite content to concentrate on her singing and dancing. It's been two years since her last LP, *Never For Ever*, and though the single that followed, 'Sat In Your Lap', reached number eleven, the recent commercial failure of 'The

Dreaming' has seen the undertakers beginning to shuffle and murmur impatiently. Her new LP, *The Dreaming*, should keep the vultures at bay however. Drawing on far greater depths of emotion and a much wider range of cultural references from Australian art to forties B-movies — it is an indication of her coming of age, both artistically and professionally."

The Dreaming was reviewed in the *Liverpool Echo* in September 1982; "Considering she produced the album herself, this is an especially pleasing fourth album for her fans. The quaint, the quiet and the queersome all inlaid on vinyl adventures in sound as on the title cut, of the intriguing 'Sat In Your Lap' or the bouncing baby, 'Suspended In Gaffa' — or the subtle and refined touch of 'Night Of The Swallow' — to the bizarre 'Leave It Open'. I wouldn't call it a challenging album, but one that shows her developing style to the full, and hints that there is still something better to come."

It was considered in *New Musical Express* in October 1982; "*The Dreaming* is an ornate, billowing record. Its songs are peculiarly ambitious: their grand design all but drives out the spirit of lowly pop music. The ghosts of famous men pace their dark corridors; great tunnels of sound emulate mighty and multi-levelled conceptions. Songs are sung in a multitude of voices, like a chittering, half-heard spirit-world. Bush's operatic entreaties are finally matched to music of a similar size and shape."

The Dreaming was reviewed in *Melody Maker* in September 1982; "Under the premise that the Great British public instinctively turns its nose up at anything that's a little unexpected, or which doesn't meet its carefully coiffured preconceptions, then this album will be an overwhelming flop. The people will be guided in their dismissive diagnosis, of course, by the all-wise radio producers who will flick quickly through it for the new 'Man With The Child In His Eyes', fail to find it, assume Kate's gone off her trolley, and make a grab for the safety of Haircut One Hundred. Reputedly two years in the making, the first album produced by Kate herself, no expense or musical craving spared, the result is mind-boggling. Even by the mannered, eccentric standards she's set herself, this is still an odd one; you may have thought 'Babooshka' and 'The Wedding List' on *Never For Ever* a little weird, then 'Get Out Of My House' and 'Houdini' here are positively manic. Always an artist of extremes, Bush has allowed her highly theatrical imagination to run riot, indulging all her musical fantasies, following her rampant instincts, and layering this album with an astonishing array of shrieks and shudders. Initially it is bewildering, if not a little preposterous, but try to hang on through the twisted overkill and the historic fits and there's much reward, if only in the sense of danger she constantly courts. Consider the options for a glamorous girl singer with an acute sense of melody; consider that she's taken the riskiest, most uncommercial route; and consider whether this album should be regarded with patience and admiration, even when it occasionally slips right over the top. Two of its ingredients, 'Sat In Your Lap' and 'The Dreaming', have already been issued as singles and sunk without a trace, which is not only significant but tragic. 'The Dreaming' is the perfect example of the passion for percussive torrents that's overtaken her (and the influence of African music?) yet it's one of her more restrained vocal performances on the album where her dynamic singing is one of the prime features ('Get Out Of My House' has her roaring and ranting like a caged lion, 'Leave It Open' has her yelling like a demented mynah bird)."

The review continued; "Elsewhere, on 'Houdini' and 'All The Love', she'll break us in gently, even tenderly, before the fuse runs out and we reel in awe and amazement at the sheer power of her rage. There's only one even vaguely conventional track, the lively 'Suspended In Gaffa', though there's something strangely disconcerting even about that and the only light track is 'There Goes A Tenner', which is even mildly funny as Kate relates a tale of skulduggery with an exaggerated cockney swagger. The lyrics, naturally, are another thing altogether. An analyst would surely come up with an interesting conclusion for her obsession with lurid drama, so vivid and colourful it could be traditional balladry. 'There Goes A Tenner' is about crime; 'Pull Out The Pin' is a graphic account of terrorism and war; 'All The Love' and 'Houdini' blaze in one different aspect of death, the latter in a particularly complex but clever way. Personally I reckon the girl watches too many B-movies. The epic track, though, the cornerstone of the album is 'Night Of The Swallow', which shows both her growing maturity as a writer and her arrival as an outstanding producer. Another complicated song (surprise, surprise) it moves gracefully through many changing moods and patterns; it's a work of both beauty and anguish, poignancy and eeriness. These twists of mood are enhanced by the use of sublime Irish music (Liam O'Flynn and Donal Lunny of Planxty, Sean Keane of the Chieftans) intersected with the rugged main action. Like most of the other tracks, I'm still not entirely sure what the hell's going on or what it's all about, but the puzzle's intriguing enough to entice you back until you unravel it. It's the sort of album that makes me want to kidnap the artist and demand the explanation and inspiration behind each track. If you're out there, Kate, do me a favour and give me a bell, huh?"

The Dreaming is just as bold and angry as it is exuberant and upbeat. From the very moment of the opening track, 'Sat In Your Lap', it becomes apparent that the days of 'Wuthering Heights' were very much behind Kate by this point in her career. And yet, there is still a range of features on the album that link it back to her previous three; there is still the romance, perception and creativity that was there in abundance on *The Kick Inside*, *Lionheart* and *Never For Ever*.

The Dreaming encapsulates all of those qualities within a framework of musical expansion and challenge, both for Kate in terms of her musical explorations as well as the listener. It was considered in *Poppix* in summer 1982; "The multi-talented skills of one of Britain's finest female performers, Kate Bush, are to be found on her new album. Entitled *The Dreaming*, the album is a departure in style from Kate's three previous albums, but in quality it remains at its usual high standard. The album pulls no punches. It's as mysterious as its name, as striking as its cover picture and as powerful as its first track, 'Sat In Your Lap'. However, probably the most interesting song on the album is its title track, 'The Dreaming'. Unfortunately, it wasn't a great commercial success, as it wasn't really picked up on by the radio stations, but it certainly warranted genuine critical acclaim for being one of the more original singles of 1982."

Each song on *The Dreaming* is an individual episode and yet musically, they all work well together in the context of the whole LP. Like a lot of music that is labelled under categories such as "art rock" and "progressive rock", *The Dreaming* is one of those albums that perhaps requires more work from the listener. Kate was quoted in 1982; "I think it (*The Dreaming*) needs two or three listens. What I wanted to do throughout the album was almost to bury things. I wanted it to be a very human, emotional album. I think we've come so far in making music sophisticated that we're almost in danger of losing the roots. That's why I think there's been a return to tribal influences. After all, that's where rock 'n' roll came from in the first place. It's a very ethnic album, as well, in many respects."

On the TV show *Pebble Mill At One* in October 1982, in response to the interviewer's statement of "On 'The Dreaming' you have Rolf Harris with his didgeridoo and you had Percy Edwards doing the animal voices and very complex lyrics and a change of voices on your part and I think that probably was the problem," Kate replied; "I think it was a very complicated single in many ways. It was demanding as much from the audience as anything that they would give the time to listen to it and try to understand it. So many people said to me that by the fifth, sixth time that they'd heard the song that they were actually starting to really like it and before then they just hadn't understood it at all. So, yeah."

When asked if she was concerned about losing fans due to *The Dreaming* not being the most accessible album, Kate told *Sounds*; "Yeah, I do, because obviously from a purely financial point of view I depend on money to make albums, and if they're not successful it's quite likely I won't have the scope to do what I want on the next one. But, I'd rather go artistically the way I want to than hang onto an audience, because you have to keep doing what you feel. It's just luck if you can hang onto the people as well... I wanted it to be a long-lasting album, because my favourite records are the ones that grow on you — that you play lots of times because each time you hear something different."

In *Zigzag* Kate said; "I don't know how they're going to take it. I think the people who've understood where I've been so far are going to be into it. They're expecting something different each time, so it's almost predictable in that respect. But I think a load of people won't like it. They probably won't understand what it's about. I find the more I write the stuff, the less I worry about this stage, and the better it is. I remember on the second and third albums there were lots of times when I was writing a song and I kept thinking what people were going to think of it. I'd rather not do that and lose some of the people who are into my music, because I'm really doing what I want to do. I'm going where I want and I'm going to keep going for it. I've no idea what's going to happen... On the last album I felt like I was starting to get there, that power thing, it was starting to get into a deeper area. A number of songs on the album were still like commercial ditties. This is the first one I feel like I've actually got somewhere. Already I'm starting to hear things that I think I could do better."

To regard *The Dreaming* as an album that demands more work from the listener isn't an attempt to elevate its musical status (music doesn't have to be complex and unusual to be good!) but equally, perhaps *The Dreaming* is an album that requires an open mind to be enjoyed for of course, it wasn't until Kate's next album, *Hounds Of Love*, that the reviewers welcomed her music back for having a more commercially friendly sound.

Besides, in favour of *The Dreaming*, it embodies what many fans love about Kate's music — it is unapologetically different and frankly, in a league of its own. Then of course, there is the fact that *The Dreaming* started to ease the door open for Kate with a wider US audience. Paul Hardiman was quoted in *Uncut* in January 2012; "EMI were probably confused by the results. It sold okay, but more importantly it registered in the US and set up the recording and production of *Hounds Of Love*." Kate said in *Sounds*; "The thing is, when I have subject-matter, the best way I could explain it would be across ten pages of foolscap, but as I've got to get it in a song, I have to précis everything. Maybe the album is more difficult for people than I meant it to be. It isn't intended to be complicated, but it obviously is, for some. A lot of it is to do with the fact that the songs are very involved — there's lots of different layers. Hopefully the next one will be simpler, but each time it gets harder, because I'm getting more involved. I'm trying to do something better all the time."

In 1985, a Canadian TV show called *The New Music* ran a feature on *Hounds Of Love*. In it, reference was made to *The Dreaming* whereby the presenter said, "The *Hounds Of Love* record represents a return to the gentler tones for which Kate Bush is most admired. To many people, *The Dreaming* has been inaccessible, her singing abrasive."

Kate said of *The Dreaming* in the same interview; "I think the last album is very dark and about pain and negativity, and the way that people treat each other badly. It was a sort of cry really and I think that perhaps the biggest influence on the last album was the fact that I was producing it so I could actually do what I wanted for the first time. And then there are a lot of things we wanted to experiment with and I particularly wanted to play around with my voices, because there are a lot of different backing vocals and things like that. The different textures were important to me. I wanted to try and create pictures with the sounds by using effects."

There doesn't seem to be any throwaway tracks on *The Dreaming*; each of them are very strong thematically and they all tell a story. In such regard, the album contains no filler. Kate said in *Sounds*; "Although there's a lot going on in some of the tracks, to me they're kept on a simple basic level within themselves — all the ideas are aiming towards the same picture. Like, some people have said it's "over-produced", but I don't think it is, because I know what I was trying to get at. I think of over-produced albums as the ones that have strings, brass, choirs, that sort of thing."

Kate said of the songs on BBC Radio One in 1982; "I think they are quite individual really. They're all about different subject matter, so there isn't really a theme, no."

She said on BBC Radio Two in September 1982; "What's nice really, because each song is slightly different, I've been able to use lots of different people to do their thing on the track.

And it was nice, because the last single had a very Australian flavour, so we used a lot of Australian sounding instruments... I've been using some different string arrangers, which is nice. I used a man called Dave Lawson and what's nice about him is he's worked a lot in film music and so he's very visually inspired. And it's nice to work with someone that's used to working with visuals as opposed to just audio. And I used a choirboy on one track — that was very nice. I've never worked with children, before, really. And he was beautiful, he was really perfect."

Despite the subject matters explored in the likes of 'Pull Out The Pin' and the title track, was *The Dreaming* a politically motivated album? Apparently not. Kate said; "It's almost an instinctive thing in white man to wipe out a race that actually owns the land. It's happening all around the world... If people have strong opinions, then they're so deep-rooted that you'll never be able to do much. Even if you can change the way a few people think, you'll never be able to change the situation anyway. I don't ever write politically, because I know nothing about politics. To me they seem more destructive than helpful. I think I write from an emotional point of view, because even though a situation may be political, there's always some emotional element, and that's what gets to me."

She was quoted in *Keyboard* in July 1985; "I always feel that the Tolkien, fantastical images seem to suggest that they're not based in reality, which I can't help but feel that a lot of my stuff is. Not all of it, but a majority is based in reality rather than fantasy. A lot of people say this, and I can't help but feel that the first two albums set that impression. You know, the feel of the production, the high voice, they sort of had a floating feel about them. But few of those songs weren't based in reality... My motivations are not social or political. It's an emotional motivation, where I'm so moved by something that's happening that I have to write about it. Apart from a few artists, I think that's how most of us feel about it. We're not necessarily politically minded. Myself, I'm not at all. I find politics extremely destructive. I see very few good, long term productive things being done by politics. It's one of those things that seems theoretically very sound, but practically, it must be an impossibility. I think that's just an emotional situation. Like nuclear war is a political thing, but it's also incredibly emotional, because it means we could all be blown up. And no one wants to be blown up. That's basic. The reason that you have to care about politics is because of how bad people are to each other."

Hmmm... Nobody lives in a vacuum though — that is to say that there is perhaps such a fine line between when something is offering a political commentary and when it isn't. For instance, with regards to a track from *Never For Ever*, Kate told *New Musical Express* in October 1982; "There was a point in people's lives when the imminent prospect of war was scaring the shit out of them, and that resulted in a lot of anti-war songs. At that time it was worthwhile. When I wrote 'Breathing' it seemed like people were sitting waiting for a nuclear bomb to go off. Nuclear power seemed like, someone was getting set to blow us up without our consent. I felt I wanted to write a song about it. If it was something that was bothering so many people then yes, I think it was worthwhile. Songs or films or little individuals don't do anything on a big level. Big things need bigger things to change them. There're loads of things I think about writing songs about which are too negative. There wouldn't be any point. They'd be too destructive and negative. And there're things which are too personal. I get loads of ideas that don't make me go, 'Ugh!', so I don't write about them. If I hear something I like, and I wish that my work could be like that because it sounds better, then it does influence me. Everything

I like and respect I suppose I move towards. It's hard to be specific when we don't know what pop music is. "Pop" is just short for popular — it could even be popular classical music."

She told *New Musical Express* in October 1982; "It would really worry me if I thought my art was being untruthful. Being true to something is the closest way to express things. But then in another way, the whole thing is untruthful — I'm being someone I'm not; I'm writing about situations I'll probably never be in. Behind it there has to be sincerity. Insincerity doesn't ring right; it has a nasty taste… I am expressing myself, but it's also something else — it's something that's coming through me. My intentions are to put across situations that aren't that close to me but which are more interesting."

Perhaps some of the negative reception directed at *The Dreaming* was derived from the fact that the album moved so far away from what Kate's public image was when she shot to fame in 1978 as the demure young woman who often spoke of home and her parents in interviews. For instance, in *Sounds* in September 1978 she was described as "sweet little Kate Bush" and in *New Musical Express* in March 1979 as "cuddly and submissive".

In an interview for BBC Radio Two in September 1982, Kate was introduced in a way that made it clear that she was still best known for 'Wuthering Heights'; "Well it was number one for quite a few weeks back in 1978, a song called 'Wuthering Heights' and it certainly launched the name of Kate Bush all over the world. It established her as an instant international success. And today, well, Kate Bush brings out a brand new album. Her story, I suppose, has been told many times, everybody knows what a tremendous success she's been. And the new album on your shelves today is called *The Dreaming*."

When asked if she felt disconcerted about the image that people perhaps had of her, Kate said in *Sounds* in October 1982;

"Oh yeah, and it worries me a bit, too. That image was something that was created in the first two years of my popularity, though, when people latched onto the fact that I was young and female, rather than a young female singer/songwriter. Now it's much easier for females to be recognised as that, because there are more around, but when I started there was really only me and Debbie Harry, and we got tied into the whole body thing. It was very flattering, but not the ideal image I would have chosen... I've spent so much time trying to prove to those people that there's more to me than that. Just the fact that I'm still around and my art keeps happening should convince them. I can't go around all the time telling people where I'm at now. I just have to hope that there are people who see the changes and change with me. I think it was just that the media didn't know how to handle it, because it was so unusual at the time... I felt that because I was so young people weren't taking me seriously. They couldn't accept that I could be so involved in what I was doing. I was very lucky, because when I left school I knew what I wanted to do, and it worked out; and I suppose I did grow up fairly fast, because in a way, I was working in an area two or three years ahead of myself."

She told *New Musical Express* in October 1982; "There're so many females that don't fit in any category at all. There're a lot of people that would love to pin them in those categories. When an image is created around a person — especially a female — there're so many presumptions thrown in. There are a lot of female artists who are stereotypes, and who nearly fall into those niches people talk about, but there are a lot who don't. When you mention traditional females it sounds as though they have nothing within them — epitomes of a situation. Any singer is a human being working inside and letting all kinds of different energies come out. The labelling that comes with the creation of an image is always a disadvantage. When someone has done something very artistic, it won't be let out when they've been packaged. When a female is attractive — whether she emphasises it or not — she's automatically projected with sexual connotations. I don't think that happens so readily with me. When I started, it seemed that a lot of singers were singing as if they weren't even related to the lyrics. They'd sing about heartbreak, and keep a big smile on their faces. For me, the singer is the expression of the song. An image should be created for each song, or at least each record; the personality that goes with that particular music. But I don't think that will ever be seen by the majority of people who look at the pictures and see the so-called images come out. When I was first happening, the only other female on the level I was being promoted at was Blondie. We were both being promoted on the basis of being female bodies as well as singers. I wasn't looked at as being a female singer/songwriter. People weren't even generally aware that I wrote my own songs or played the piano until maybe a year or so after that. The media just promoted me as a female body. It's like I've had to prove that I'm an artist inside a female body. The idea of the body as a vehicle is just one of those things. But I'm someone who talks about music and song."

It is apparent that even from the beginning of her career, Kate was keen to do things in a way that best suited her artistic aspirations. Under her own initiative, she opted to have the dance lessons with Lindsay Kemp that would ultimately inspire her use of movement, as made iconic in the 'Wuthering Heights' video.

Kate always resisted EMI trying to urge her to write songs that were more commercial and it was her who insisted against an early promotional campaign that put more emphasis on her appearance than on her music. She even had the final say on which of her songs would be released as a debut single (EMI initially wanted to go with 'James And The Cold Gun' rather than 'Wuthering Heights'). When asked if there was ever any conflict between herself and the record company when it came to choosing which songs to release as singles, Kate explained on BBC Radio Two in September 1982; "I think that situation differs greatly from artist to artist and in my situation I'm very lucky, I seem to normally have the last say in which the single will be."

Kate said on BBC Radio Two in 1982; "I was very young. I was sixteen, still at school, and I had no experience in the business at all. And I think in a way all of us wanted to just hang on until I was a bit more prepared to cope with the situation. And as far as I'm concerned I'm very glad that did happen, because in those two years between leaving school and things starting to happen when the album was released, I really built a foundation for myself as a person as well as for the direction I was going in. Since I left school I was going to London every day and to dancing classes and really for the first time becoming an individual. And I think those couple of years were really important."

Interestingly, whether it was from the press or from herself, intentionally or not, there has often been a strong link made between Kate Bush as an artist and Kate Bush as a person. Across a range of sources, people have often attempted to link her songs to what may have been going on in her life at the time. Kate said in *Sounds*; "There are certain parts of me that definitely don't want to look at reality. Generally speaking, though, I'm quite realistic, but perhaps the songs on the first two albums created some kind of fantasy image, so people presumed that I lived in that kind of world."

She told *Melody Maker*; "From a writing point of view I think you are talking about something that is very real-based but sometimes to make it more interesting you have to exaggerate it a little bit. It's like people who tell stories, really the people who tell good stories are the ones who kept the truth in essence but they exaggerate on all the little areas."

Elsewhere she said; "I don't think I am eccentric as a person. When I get older I might be. Maybe my music is a little eccentric sometimes. People can react as seriously as they want to. I'd like them to sit there with the lyrics in front of them and the record turned up really loud, giving themselves to it. A lot of people will listen to it, and a certain percentage will take time and effort to get into it."

Of course, the abrasive nature of *The Dreaming* should definitely not overshadow the grace of the artist behind the work. Kate said on BBC Radio One in 1982; "When I went to Canada, years ago, I was doing a whole day of interviews with journalists and there was a lady journalist, and we only sat and chatted for about thirty minutes. And when I first met her, I said 'your earrings are beautiful.' And when she left she took them off and gave them to me, and said, 'I hope they bring you luck'."

It comes across that Kate was often keen to credit good interviewers accordingly. In an interview on German radio in 1982, she said; "I was saying to a journalist today that all the interviews I've done today in Munich were incredible. The questions were very clever, very precise, they'd done all their research, they knew a lot, and I really enjoyed talking to them. The standard was incredible and compared to the English press, on average it was just superb, wonderful... I love to talk about my music because that's what I love. It gets very boring for me to sit and talk about myself all the time."

The instrumentation used on *The Dreaming* is significantly unique and at times it creates sounds that clash and can be overall, jarring. Good. It is clear that this wasn't an album designed to be "pretty" or something that could be listened to for the purpose of relaxation. It was considered in the *Village*

Voice in April 1983 that "the revelation is the dense, demanding music" and that the album is "the most impressive Fripp/Gabriel-style art-rock album of the post-punk refulgence."

So is *The Dreaming* an essential album? Well, I guess it depends how you look at it. As a Kate Bush fan, it is absolutely essential because it documents a fascinating phase in her career where there was a strong emphasis on a change of musical direction. But is the album essential for those who are less invested in following Kate Bush's career? Yes, in terms of its unique character and the musical exploration it offers as part of that but truthfully, no if you're looking for something that you can sing along to.

As anxious as I am to say that as a Kate Bush fan, I would argue that a lot of the appeal of *The Dreaming* is that it is so flipping different: And that's okay — it was designed to be. It is abrasive, noisy and it is a lot to take on board. *The Dreaming* is impressive in its ability to overwhelm. It goes beyond, if you will, "songs".

Whilst weirdness doesn't immediately make something a good album, Kate's strength as a writer and as a creative innovator shines through. Besides, the sheer eccentricity of *The Dreaming* it is an excellent vehicle through which Kate was able to take her talents in a new direction — considering the eccentricity of all of her albums prior to *The Dreaming*, could anything less have really been expected?

There were of course, certainly moments of shade and light on *The Dreaming*. Although the overall thing feels "noisy", there are still moments of contrast. The interviewer commented on how there is good use of silence and space on *The Dreaming*, to which Kate said in *Electronics & Music Maker* in October 1982; "I've begun to value silence much more because I think even from the start I realised silence is as important as the notes. But actually getting your songs to realise that is so much harder, and also knowing where to put the silence. Again, this album is probably the first one that has actually let silence into it. The bass lines are kept fairly "dry", which helps, too. And my piano playing is never over-busy. It probably couldn't be, though, my technique holds me back quite a lot there! I use the synthesiser for things that I definitely want to hear, so I will specifically ask for that. But again in a lot of cases, maybe I've asked them to do something, and while they're mucking around I'll pick on another sound that's so good we'll go with that."

So was making *The Dreaming* a positive experience for Kate Bush? And what of how she felt about how the album was received? Well, to be honest, as much as other writings on her work have attempted to make an assessment of this, I don't think it is anyone's place to.

But was there an encouraging working rapport between those involved on the album? It would seem to be the case. In response to the question of how she keeps her confidence in a good place when working on new material, Kate said on BBC Radio One in 1982; "It's down to the people you're working with, 'cause if you've got a positive vibe happening between the team, then really if it starts going negative you can just pull it away, you can say to the people 'look, come on, you know, let's forget about that.' And I really think it is down to the relationship and the feelings between the people you're working with, and I was really lucky because all the people I work with are really great, they're fantastic... I don't think I'm very positive sometimes, I think I'm quite negative at times, you know. But I think there's always the feeling in me that there's no reason for me to be negative because everything's great, so why be negative? And then I feel better."

She said in *New Musical Express*; "You gauge by feedback as to whether your voice inside is right. It says 'Do this,' and you have to see what other people say about it. The barrier against self-indulgence has to come from within yourself. You have to see other people's criticism to be able to do anything about it. You can get a different answer to a problem from everyone you know."

She told *Company* in January 1982; "I find that I now rely much more on other people's feedback, especially when I lack confidence about a song."

Nick Launay was quoted in *Uncut* in January 2012; "Very often she'd come to do the take and each time she'd play the song slightly differently. It wouldn't be a case of the musicians getting annoyed, it would be a case of people laughing, rolling on the floor, saying to her, 'No, no, when you get to that bit you're doing something different...' I did a lot of editing together of different takes and it got very confusing at times. I don't think she had any realisation of how complex songs like 'The Dreaming' were. To her they were very simple."

Kate told *New Musical Express*; "Since it all started for me, it hasn't stopped. I'd no idea what was going to happen. I've no regrets in starting that way, in getting through so quickly — because you have to keep fighting anyway, and it made things quicker, not easier. If I hadn't got the encouragement I did, I don't know. I might not have had so much faith, really. Less confidence in getting involved. But it gets harder. Each time you do something you have all the knowledge and mistakes behind you, so you know more: you have more to think about. I have to create time to write now. I don't stop working. I haven't really stopped since I began. If this album hadn't sold well, I'd still carry on in this direction. If I made a record which I didn't much like and it sold well, I'd still want to change the direction. When you're making an expression of yourself, you have to be happy with it. To do it and keep getting better — that's so hard. I travelled constantly for the first two years of my career. Much of it was incredibly sheltered, in that I only saw hotels,

TV studios and aeroplanes. The few times that I've travelled on a social level have brought me minimal knowledge, really, about other places. I think I've learned more from the people than from the places."

And who wouldn't want to be in a supportive working environment having reached such a level of fame? Upon being asked how she felt about people doing impressions of her, Kate said in an interview with BBC Radio One; "I think I have second thoughts about my performance anyway. I think that just exaggerates the point. But it's great, I love to watch the way that they do it. It's very fun."

Kate still found being famous surreal at times. "It comes from seeing just how much I have done over the last three years, she told *Company* in January 1982. "Sometimes I find it hard to understand people's interest in me. I hate it when I feel that someone is just after the scandalous details. The most important part of my life is my work."

Elsewhere she said; "There's been such a lot written about me by people who say they know me, but who I've never met. I find that a great intrusion, a kind of violation."

She told the *Newcastle Evening Chronicle* in September 1980; "I think the public have become conditioned to want to know who is sleeping with who, or how many marriages somebody has had, but as far as I'm concerned, it's totally irrelevant. I'm really very normal and there is nothing sensational to uncover. I wouldn't talk about some private things to my mother so why should I to anybody else?"

In response to the fact that she found her initial success difficult to handle, Kate said in *Sounds*; "I still find some things frightening. I've adjusted a hell of a lot, but it still scares me. There are so many aspects that if you start thinking about are terrifying. The best thing to do is not even to think about them. Just try to sail through."

So how had success affected her working process? "I've become a perfectionist, for one thing... I wasn't a daydreamer. Writing songs and poetry is putting into words and music my real feelings. Without being too critical of 'Wuthering Heights', I do think that it was a bit misleading — it seemed to suggest too much fantasy and escapism... I think my lyrics have a far tougher edge to them now. I always thought that ultimately I would be super tough, presuming that as I gathered experiences I would learn to accept situations for what they are. That has worked in some ways, but in others I'm far more vulnerable."

Kate said in *Keyboard* in July 1985; "It's always the song that tells you what to do. In my head, I'm thinking that I'm finished with this, but the song will go, 'Look, you can't get this if you don't do this...' The song is controlling you. It tells you what to do really. If it works, great. If it doesn't, it just keeps you dragging along behind it. It's strange... Quite often, I get the lyrics and melody in a short burst. Maybe I'll get the first verse or the choruses straight away. Then it'll take me forever just trying to piece the rest together, because you have to try to maintain a level of quality within the lyrics, especially if you're trying to tell a story. You have to get the phrasing right, but you're hoping your audience will be able to see where you're going. I find that the most difficult thing to do, especially if it's something like *The Dreaming*, which I found totally interesting. It was very difficult for me to do that and get across what I wanted. Some of the songs really do take me a very long time, although perhaps the initial ideas came rather quickly... Sometimes the backing vocals just come in automatically as part of a song when I'm writing it. Other times, maybe it won't be until I've recorded the main voice and a few events in the song. And then I'll think it needs something there. Those are really the two extremes: I either come up with the backing vocals in the initial writing, or I hear a hole that needs filling.

Whether I build up a really thick, grand vocal depends on the song. If the song needs that, then I'll just overdub the voice and build the vocals up. If it's a very intimate song between the singer and the subject matter, then you'd write it with just one voice."

Endearingly, there was always something to aim for. Kate told *Company* in January 1982 that what was most important to her, was "to feel that I am progressing with my own life and my work. I also desperately want to feel some kind of happiness in what I am creating. Not contentment, but pleasure... I always feel that I can try harder. I always feel that there isn't enough time in this life to achieve all the things that I want... I suppose that if the day ever came when I was one hundred percent satisfied, that would be the day that I stopped growing and changing."

She said in *Poppix* in summer 1982; "It's very important for me to change. In fact, as soon as the songs began to be written, I knew that the album was going to be quite different. I'd hate it, especially now, if my albums became similar, because so much happens to me between each album — my views change quite drastically. What's nice about this album is that it's what I've always wanted to do. For instance, the Australian thing: well, I wanted to do that on the last album, but there was no time. There are quite a few ideas and things that I've had whizzing around in my head that just haven't been put down. I've always wanted to use more traditional influences and instruments, especially the Irish ones. I suppose subconsciously I've wanted to do all this for quite some time, but I've never really had the time until now... Although on the first two albums the songs were always based on something, they weren't all that strong; but now I get more involved with the ideas behind a song, and I do my best to make the concept as vivid and as solid as I can. On the new album, for instance, there is a track about the legendary escapologist Houdini. During his incredible lifetime Houdini took it upon himself to expose the whole spiritualist thing — you know, séances and mediums... I thought that was so beautiful — the idea that this man who had spent his life escaping from chains and ropes had actually managed to contact his wife. The image was so beautiful that I just had to write a song about it."

When asked how she felt about her early records, Kate said to *Sounds*; "I don't really like them. A lot of the stuff on the first two albums I wasn't at all happy with. I think I'm still fond of a lot of the songs, but I was unhappy about the way they came across on record. Also, until this album (*The Dreaming*) I'd never really enjoyed the sound of my own voice. It's always been very difficult for me, because I've wanted to hear the songs in a different way... I think a lot of people don't like the sound of their own voices. It's like you have to keep working towards something you eventually do like. It was very satisfying for me on this album, because for the first time I can sit and listen to the vocals and think, 'Yeah, that's actually quite good.'... I probably used to push it more in other ways. I went through a phase of trying to leap up and down a lot when I was writing songs. I used to try to push it almost acrobatically. Now I'm trying more to get the song across, and I have more control. When I'm trying to think up the character is when it needs a bit of push."

It's important not to forget that the way in which Kate was embraced by the public at the start of her career was a strong catalyst for getting the ball rolling towards further creativity. She said in *Poppix*; "Since 1978, when everything really started happening to me, with 'Wuthering Heights' reaching number one and the British Rock and Pop Awards, I've been very lucky in the sense that people have really helped me out. It made me feel that people were really interested in my music, and it was great. It gave me an incredible amount of courage to go for things, never to be scared of a challenge. I'm sure that if people hadn't accepted me so warmly, I would have become a more conventional performer."

As with the majority of Kate's albums, *The Dreaming* wasn't supported with a tour. Besides, time spent working on an album was time that couldn't be spent on practising dance. Kate said on Radio One; "The problem is when I'm making albums I can't dance, as well. So I have to wait until I've finished the project before I can start again. I probably do about three to four hours a day when I haven't got anything else on. The last few months I've been getting back into it. It feels a great again."

Kate said on BBC Radio Two; "For the last couple of months I've been getting back into (dance) training because while I've been making the album there's been no time at all, so I've been unfit for a whole year. And of course when you leave it alone for a length of time, coming back to it is even harder and it's very painful, you know, you can't walk for days. But it's all in preparation for things that are coming up in the future, for videos and that sort of thing. So there are a lot of areas that I have to work on all time, which is again why I seem to be so busy."

When asked on Radio One which she preferred out of "writing songs, recording, touring, working with other people on their albums, producing, or dancing," Kate replied, "I do like them all very much. But I think, definitely the priority for me is the writing of the songs. It's the most challenging, frustrating, satisfying thing there is."

And how about writing songs for other people? Kate replied: "I've never tried, but it's something that, yes, it's quite appealing. The problem is really getting time, because I normally only have enough time to scrape enough songs together myself for an album. But it's very appealing, yeah."

She said on Radio Two; "I would like to think that I'm going to stay in the singing world because I think the thing that means a lot to me — it means more than anything, really. I think I'd rather stay writing songs and singing them then anything else and if there's any way that I can continue to do that then I would love to very much. But, I must admit, dancing is another interest that perhaps I would go off on a bit more in the future, it really depends how things go for me."

Although there wasn't a tour, it is plausible that Kate was open to the possibility of doing one. When asked if a tour was in the pipeline, she said on Radio One; "I really want to and I'm going to start thinking about it before the end of this year in order to try and get something to happen before next year, 'cause it's a good six months rehearsal, really. And I'm hoping to get something together for next year, but I don't know when. As soon as I do, I'll let everyone know."

Time and money were inevitably barriers to touring. Kate said; "With forty people to look after, it was astronomical — but it was worth it. Well yes, I've made money, but a lot of that money goes into projecting my art."

In August 1982, she said on Radio One; "I really do want to do another tour, badly. But, well, from the way the last one was it just cost so much money and so much effort and time to get it together, that it needs an incredible amount of preparation, really. I'm just trying to see when is the first time that I can realistically fit it in."

Kate told *Poppix* in summer 1982; "The last tour was so much effort, and it cost so much money, and we actually spent about four months rehearsing for it, so the thought of another one is a little bit daunting. It's such a big thing to commit yourself to — it's like a whole year taken out of your life. It scares me a bit."

She told *Company*; "The worst thing is not being prepared; I have to know, before I go on stage, exactly what I am going to do. Rehearsals may take hours but they have to be done."

The amount of thought and work that Kate had put into her 1979 tour was such that further tours were not something that she would have wanted to embark on half-heartedly. She said on Radio Two; "I'm probably not as nervous before I go on stage for a concert as I am for a lot of other things. The great thing about the show we did, for instance, was we rehearsed it for so long that there was very little to be that nervous of, because it was so rehearsed. In fact, it was quite a relief to do it for the first night because it was actually going out to an audience. But I think I do suffer from nerves a lot in other areas, and I worry a lot, especially about, is my music good enough at the moment, am I really doing the right thing, is this good enough, is that good enough. And I think it is all quite tied in with nerves so I do get nervous in situations where things are very important. But, I think you learn to cope. But sometimes I'm a lot less nervous about some things now than I used to be on other things. I mean, I still get nervous for instance, like speaking on the radio, but it's not as nerve-racking for me as it would have been a couple of years ago. And yet other things seem to get even more worrying for me. One of the hardest things I find to do, is get up in a room full of people and just speak to them. I think that is incredibly difficult… I've been dying to do some more performances since the last show and I'm really hoping to get something together next year. My problem is that it really takes so much time that there's no way we could fit it in this year. And as yet I don't know when it will be next year, but it will be next year sometime... There are so many different areas. It's really like a huge, great jigsaw that you're piecing together. You have to start with a band, and then you have the people that are up front like the dancers, you have the lighting guy, the stage designer, the costumes, the crew, a tour manager, there are just so many areas. And in a lot of ways, because it's dance and sound, I'm involved in a lot of those fringe areas as well. And it really would take a good six months to get another tour together... We like to go for a theatrical show."

Go big or go home. In response to the interviewer's comment that for a tour, a lot of people would be happy to just see Kate sitting at a piano and singing a set of songs, she said in *New Musical Express*; "It would be too easy, as if I couldn't be bothered to prepare a proper show. It wouldn't do anything for the blend of movement and music. That is what I really want to do. Music and movement together in a modern sense. People like it that you're not taking the easy way out."

It is plausible that if time was an unlimited resource, Kate would have done a lot of performances across a range of areas. "I want to get into films. And I want to do more on stage," she said to *Company*. "I love staging my own shows, working out the routines, designing the whole package, and using every aspect of my creativity... My favourite film is *Don't Look Now*. I was incredibly impressed by the tension, the drive and the way that every loose end was tied up. I get so irritated by films which leave ideas hanging."

Kate told *Melody Maker*; "I think it's the album I'm most happy with that I've completed. I went through all the problems and depression during the album and then ended up feeling quite pleased with it. In the past it's worked the other way around."

Years later, it seems that Kate herself didn't relate to *The Dreaming* anymore. She was quoted in *Q* in December 1993; "I look back at that record and it seems mad. I heard it about three years ago and couldn't believe it. There's a lot of anger in it. There's a lot of 'I'm an artist, right!'"

The emotion that Kate put into *The Dreaming* was perhaps

very much of its time in terms of where she was at with her career when she made the album. She said in *New Musical Express*; "The worst thing? The pressures, I suppose. They come in from so many different levels — from so many people — that they feel destructive towards me as a human being. Although it happens very rarely. And I have so little time to do things I want to... It scares me that I work too hard. I can be so tired and involved in work that I'm not living on another level. It's a reality of the situation. I have to do things I don't want to, so that I can do what I want the rest of the time. It's that I don't seem to have time to myself."

It is understandable as to how Kate may have been keen to have a break by the end of 1982. She said in the *Liverpool Echo* in October 1985; "It's difficult when you've been working for years producing one album after another. You need fresh things to stimulate you. My actions seemed to worry other people more than they did me. I didn't care about being out of the limelight for a spell because I've never been interested in fame for fame's sake... The pop scene is incredibly bitchy. When you read reports like some of these about yourself, you feel so vulnerable. I'm a private person and when I'm working in my studio I prefer to live an isolated lifestyle and not be treated like somebody famous. In fact, when I emerge back out into the real world afterwards, and people begin giving me the star treatment, it always makes me feel very strange."

Hard work reaped artistic rewards though. Regarding his time working on *The Dreaming*, Paul Hardiman was quoted in *Uncut* in January 2012; "Working on the album was hours of crippling tedium with bursts of extreme excitement. At times Kate was just exhausted. It was hard work, but hugely rewarding."

In 2011, Björk listed *The Dreaming* as one of her favourite albums, as did Big Boi in 2013. Steven Wilson also stated that as well as *The Dreaming* being one of his favourite albums, it was also a key influence for his 2015 album, *Hand. Cannot. Erase.*

Some may say that *The Dreaming* — both in terms of production and from a musical perspective — set Kate up for her next album, *Hounds Of Love*. During the creation of the latter, in an interview with *Keyboard* in July 1985, Kate was asked, "Is the album you're working on going to be a departure from *The Dreaming*, or is it a continuation of the ideas you developed there?" Her response: "It's difficult for me to say, really. I think it is different from *The Dreaming*. When I sit down and write songs for a new album, that's one of the things that's important to me — that it's at least somehow different and hopefully interesting."

Well, *The Dreaming* was certainly different and interesting and in the context of Kate Bush's entire career, it is a fascinating insight into where she was with things creatively at the time. After all, each of her albums have always been a step forward in terms of musical exploration and *The Dreaming* ranks right up there in that regard.

The Dreaming
A Comprehensive Discography

Personnel

Musicians

Kate Bush — vocals, piano (exc. 4), programming, electronic drums, Fairlight CMI synthesiser (1, 2, 5–10), Yamaha CS-80 (2), strings (4)

Paddy Bush — sticks (1), mandolins and strings (4), bullroarer (6)

Geoff Downes — Fairlight CMI trumpet section (1)

Jimmy Bain — bass guitar (1, 5, 10)

Del Palmer — bass guitar (2, 4, 8), fretless and 8 string bass (7)

Preston Heyman — drums (1, 3, 5, 10), sticks (1)

Stuart Elliott — drums (2, 4, 6–9), sticks (4), percussion (8)

Dave Lawson — Synclavier (2, 4)

Brian Bath — electric guitar (3)

Danny Thompson — string bass (3)

Ian Bairnson — acoustic guitar (5)

Alan Murphy — electric guitar (5, 10)

Liam O'Flynn — penny whistle and uilleann pipes (7)

Seán Keane — fiddle (7)

Dónal Lunny — bouzouki (7)

Eberhard Weber — double bass (9)

Other Voices

Paddy Bush, Ian Bairnson, Stewart Arnold and Gary Hurst —
    backing vocals (1)
Paddy Bush — backing vocals (6, 10)
David Gilmour — backing vocals (3)
Percy Edwards — animals (6)
Gosfield Goers — crowd (6)
Richard Thornton — choirboy (8)
Gordon Farrell — Houdini (9)
Del Palmer — Rosabel Believe (9)
Paul Hardiman — Eeyore (10)
Esmail Sheikh — drum talk (10)

Technical

Kate Bush — producer
Paul Hardiman — recording engineer at Advision and
    Odyssey Studios, all mixes at Advision Studios
Teri Reed, David Taylor — assistant engineers
David Taylor — mixing assistant
Haydn Bendall — engineer at Abbey Road Studios
Danny Dawson and John Barrett — assistant engineers
Hugh Padgham and Nick Launay — engineer at Townhouse
    Studios
George Chambers, Howard Gray and Nick Cook — assistant
    engineers
Peter Wooliscroft — digital editing
Ian Cooper — mastering engineer

Track Listing

All tracks written, arranged and produced by Kate Bush, except the pipe and strings on 'Night Of The Swallow' which were arranged by Bill Whelan, and the strings on 'Houdini' which were arranged by Dave Lawson and Andrew Powell.

Side One
1. Sat In Your Lap (3:29)
2. There Goes A Tenner (3:24)
3. Pull Out The Pin (5:26)
4. Suspended In Gaffa (3:54)
5. Leave It Open (3:20)

Side Two
6. The Dreaming (4:41)
7. Night Of The Swallow (5:22)
8. All The Love (4:29)
9. Houdini (3:48)
10. Get Out Of My House (5:25)

Country By Country

UK
Original release, September 1982:
EMI EMC 3419, LP
TC-EMC 3419, cassette

Reissues:
CDP 7463612, CD, 1987
EMI CDP 7 46361 2, CD 1990
EMI EMC 3419, LP, 1990
Fish People FPCD002, CD, 13th May 2011
Parlophone 0190295568955, CD, 16th November 2018
Parlophone, 0190295593872 , LP, 16th November 2018

USA
Original release, September 1982:
EMI America ST-17084, LP

Reissues:
EMI America 4XT 17084 cassette, 1986
EMI America CDP 7 46361 2, CD, 1987
EMI-Manhattan Records, D 101879, CD, club edition
EMI-Manhattan Records, E4 46361, cassette
CEMA Special Markets, S11-56886, LP, 1993

Japan
Original release, 1st October 1982:
EMI EMS-91044, LP
EMI ZR28-813, cassette

Reissues:
EMI CP32-5277, CD, 25th February 1987
EMI TOCP-6702, CD, 12th April 1991

EMI TOCP-3008, CD, 31st May 1995
EMI TOCP-67818, CD, EMC 3419, 2nd November 2005
Reissued in 2008 with the same catalogue number but a different obi strip.
Fish People TOCP-71124, CD, 20th July 2011
Parlophone WPCR-80050, CD, 29th January 2014

SINGLES

UK

Sat In Your Lap / Lord Of The Reedy River
EMI EMI 5201, 18th June 1981
Released over a year before the album, the non-album B-side is a Donovan song that originally appeared on Donovan's 1971 double album *HMS Donovan*.

The Dreaming / Dreamtime (Instrumental Version)
EMI EMI 5296, 23rd July 1982

There Goes A Tenner / Ne T'Enfuis Pas
EMI EMI 5350, 29th October 1982
The b-side is a non-album track sung in French.

USA
No singles were released in the USA from the album although a 4-track 12" promotional sampler was pressed up (EMI America SPRO-9847). The four tracks were:
Suspended In Gaffa / Pull Out The Pin
Sat In Your Lap / There Goes A Tenner

Like the States, there were no singles released in Japan but there were other single couplings from around the world:

Suspended In Gaffa / Dreamtime (Instrumental)
EMI France 2C 008-64.957, 1982, France

Suspended In Gaffa / Ne T'Enfuis Pas
EMI Electrola 1C 006-64 972, 1982, Germany
Also released in Spain and in January 1983 in Australia.

Night Of The Swallow / Houdini
EMI Ireland I EMI 9001, 25th November 1983, Ireland

In-depth Series

The In-depth series was launched in March 2021 with four titles. Each book takes an in-depth look at an album; the history behind it; the story about its creation; the songs, as well as detailed discographies listing release variations around the world. The series will tackle albums that are considered to be classics amongst the fan bases, as well as some albums deemed to be "difficult" or controversial; shining new light on them, following reappraisal by the authors.

Titles to date:

Jethro Tull - Thick As A Brick	*978-1-912782-57-4*
Tears For Fears - The Hurting	*978-1-912782-58-1*
Kate Bush - The Kick Inside	*978-1-912782-59-8*
Deep Purple - Stormbringer	*978-1-912782-60-4*
Emerson Lake & Palmer - Pictures At An Exhibition	978-1-912782-67-3
Korn - Follow The Leader	978-1-912782-68-0
Elvis Costello - This Year's Model	978-1-912782-69-7
Kate Bush - The Dreaming	978-1-912782-70-3

Forthcoming:

Jethro Tull - Minstrel In The Gallery	978-1-912782-81-9
Deep Purple - Fireball	978-1-912782-82-6
Deep Purple - Slaves And Masters	978-1-912782-83-3
Talking Heads - Remain In Light	
Jethro Tull - Heavy Horses	
Rainbow - Straight Between The Eyes	
The Stranglers - La Folie	
Alice Cooper - Love It To Death	